Your H(
A Place of Grace

YOUR HOME

A Place of Grace

SUSAN HUNT

CROSSWAY BOOKS • WHEATON, ILLINOIS
A DIVISION OF GOOD NEWS PUBLISHERS

Your Home a Place of Grace

Copyright © 2000 by Susan Hunt

Published by Crossway Books
        a division of Good News Publishers
        1300 Crescent Street
        Wheaton, Illinois 60187

Cover design: Cindy Kiple

First printing 2000

Printed in the United States of America

Library of Congress Cataloging-in-Publication Data
Hunt, Susan, 1940-
    Your home a place of grace / Susan Hunt.
       p.   cm.
    ISBN 1-58134-185-7 (alk. paper)
    1. Family—Religious life. 2. Parenting—Religious aspects—
Presbyterian Church in America. 3. Child rearing—Religious aspects—
Presbyterian Church in America. 4. Covenant theology—Study and
Teaching. 5. Presbyterian Church in America—Doctrines. I. Title.
    BX8968.55.H86   2000
    248.4—dc21   00-008837
                                          CIP

15	14	13	12	11	10	09	08	07	06	05	04	03	02	01	00
15	14	13	12	11	10	9	8	7	6	5	4	3	2	1	

Our family dedicates this book
to our church families—

Midway Presbyterian Church, Marietta, Georgia
Decatur Presbyterian Church, Decatur, Alabama

These two church families embody the covenant way.
They have rejoiced with us in times of joy
and wept with us in times of sorrow.
They teach and encourage us.
They challenge and comfort us.
They love us. And we love them.
They are not perfect, but they are being perfected
by the Savior they love and serve.
We thank our God for them.
Gene and Susan Hunt (Midway)

Kathryn and Dean Barriault (Decatur)
Hunter, Mary Kate, Daniel, Susie and Sam

Richie and Shannon Hunt (Midway)
Mac and Angus

Laurin and Scott Coley (Midway)
Cassie and Scotty

Susan's mother, Mary Kathryn McLaurin (Midway)

The longing for home is woven into the fabric of the life of every man, every woman, and every child. It is profoundly affected by their inescapable connection to place, persons, and principles—the incremental parts of a covenant community. While the nomad spirit of modernity has dashed the integrity of community, it has done nothing to alter the need for it. Covenantal attachment has always been an inescapable aspect of the healthy psyche, and it always will be. Uprootedness has always been a kind of psychosis, and likewise, it always will be. Hearth and home are the cornerstones of help, hope, and happiness. . . .

Humanness cannot be found in escape, detachment, absence of commitment, or undefined freedom. Instead, its great promise may only be found in those rare places where people have established identity, defined vocation, and envisioned destiny. It comes from the sense of connection to land and people and heritage that occurs when people try to provide continuity and identity across generations. Such a commitment is inevitably costly, but that is precisely what makes home so infinitely priceless.

That kind of covenantal attachment to home simply cannot occur anywhere. It must be intentionally rooted somewhere specific, somewhere unique, somewhere preclusive, somewhere that is inherently good and right and true.

George Grant, from *Going Somewhere*

CONTENTS

ACKNOWLEDGMENTS

My family's fingerprints are on every page of this book. Our lives are so intertwined that I usually do not know where their ideas stop and mine start. The oneness that Gene and I enjoy spills over into our relationships with our children and their families. Their love, prayers, encouragement, and laughter fill my life with joy. Their practical help makes my writing possible. Mama's prayers enfold me, and her wonderful meals give me many extra hours to write.

The RaceRunner Sunday school class helped me make the decision to write this book, and they stuck by me until the last word was written. These young couples listened as I struggled to clarify the thoughts in each chapter. They provided the questions at the end of the chapters and then helped me formulate the answers to those questions. Their desire to understand the covenant way kept me focused and energized.

My colleagues at the Presbyterian Church in America Christian Education Office and the Women's Advisory Subcommittee are more than coworkers. They are friends. I am very grateful for their help and encouragement.

The people who wrote the "Tell the Next Generation" stories at the beginning of the chapters and those who share their testimonies in various chapters are beautiful reflections of grace. Their stories breathe life into this book, and I am humbled that they were willing to share the gifts and graces of their life experiences on these pages.

Dick Aeschliman, Dianne Balch, Kathryn Barriault, Sharon Betters, Lynn Brookside, Dean Conkel, Vicki Drake, Charles Dunahoo, Bob Edmiston, George and Karen Grant, Sue Jakes, Bob Palmer, Tom and Jane Patete, Paul and Georgia Settle, and Barbara Thompson read and reacted to chapters. Their wisdom is woven throughout this book.

Mrs. Rosalie Cassels is a spiritual mother who guides and encourages me. She is a true mother in Israel.

As I look over this list of people, what amazes me most is that it is essentially the same people who are listed in the acknowledgement section of every book I have written. These family members and friends have not just invested in my projects. They invest in my life. I know Jesus better and love Him more because of them.

And finally my thanks to the wonderful people at Crossway. Their integrity, commitment to excellence, and uncompromising faithfulness to the Lord are a refreshing combination. May the Lord continue to use their ministry to advance His kingdom.

INTRODUCTION

Thirty years ago if someone had asked me to write a book about the family, I would probably have thought, *It's about time!* In my youthful arrogance I was sure we knew how to create a model Christian home. We had three beautiful, well-behaved children who could recite numerous Scripture verses on command. We had family devotions, took our children to visit the sick and elderly, made cards for children of missionaries on Sunday afternoons, frequently had church members in our home, and always arrived at church scrubbed, pressed, and early. I had dozens of formulas, and it would have seemed perfectly reasonable to me that others would want to know how we did it.

I'm grateful no one asked.

Now when someone suggested that I write a book on parenting, it seemed the most preposterous thing I could imagine. I finally agreed to pray about it. What harm could that do? I was sure God knew that I have nothing to say about this topic. The one thing I have learned in thirty years of parenting is how much I do not know. Gene and I have learned that our formulas were hollow and mechanical. The plans and platitudes were sprinkled with Scripture but not seasoned with grace. Now when we pray for our children and grandchildren, more often than not we utter the prayer of Jehoshaphat: "We do not know what to do, but our eyes are upon you" (2 Chronicles 20:12).

But the more I prayed about writing this book, the more a strange and wonderful thought germinated. Perhaps, just perhaps, we need a book that does not talk about behavioral and formulaic solutions. Could it be that Jehoshaphat's prayer is in fact the answer?

Then I was struck with another reason it was preposterous to write a book on parenting. How could I possibly separate parenting from the marriage, or from the church, or from all of life?

Bingo! I couldn't. Now I was faced with another question. Could it be that the time is ripe for a return to the biblical concept of covenant?

A covenantal perspective does not divide life into neat little compartments. Thinking covenantally means that we see the wide expanse of God's mercy and grace to His children intricately woven into every relationship and detail of life, but it also means that we are comfortable not always seeing or understanding how that happens. This comfort is firmly rooted in confidence—not self-confidence but sure confidence in the person and work of Jesus Christ. A covenantal perspective is worldview thinking—seeing the connections in Scripture and the connection of Scripture to all spheres of life.

My excitement exploded. I am passionate about the biblical doctrine of the covenant, and my desire to see God's people apply this doctrine in their lives is a fire in my bones. The idea of a book that examines a covenantal perspective of the home intrigued me, but there was still a lingering question. Why should *I* write this book? The only reasonable explanation I can give is that God chooses to use "the foolish things of the world to shame the wise. . . . so that no one may boast before him" (1 Corinthians 1:27, 29).

I admit that I have moments of terror when I think about what I am doing, but turning away from this project would be even more terrifying. I cling to the promise of my Savior, "My grace is sufficient for you, for my power is made perfect in weakness," and I say with Paul, "I will boast all the more gladly about my weaknesses, so that Christ's power may rest on me" (1 Corinthians 12:9).

IT'S NOT ABOUT US

One of the many qualms I had about writing this book was that some would look at our family and conclude that we are a wonderful example of a Christian family. We have three believing children who are married to believers. They are all raising their children in the nurture and admonition of the Lord. But each of us, and anyone who knows us, will tell you that we are all a mess. Those who know us well could tell you endless stories of individual and collective weaknesses, failures, or grief that would cause any reasonable person to think this family should surely come unraveled. And these messy tales are not all past tense. They are ongoing. But the Lord has made His face shine upon us. He has been gracious to us. He has turned His face toward us and given us peace. Any glory you see is not a glory intrinsic to us. It is the reflected glory of our Creator, Redeemer, and Sustainer.

This book is not about our family. It is about the God who has claimed us for Himself.

Any Christian family is a trophy of God's grace, and all glory belongs to Him.

THE NEED

It is not necessary to catalog the statistics or the anecdotes of the cultural apologists and prognosticators regarding the crisis of the family. It would take a monumental leap of denial for us to fail to see that we are living in a post-Christian culture. The forecast for this generation of children is terrifying. Biblical truth is not the consensus of the citizenry, and we see the consequences being played out in every arena. But it seems to me that the saddest consequence is in the home, even Christian homes.

Many Christian marriages are hollow and dissonant.

Many Christian parents are panic-stricken about raising children in our postmodern culture. Many are heartbroken about choices their "good" kids have made. Many are devastated about rebellious children.

Often Christian homes are battlegrounds rather than sanctuaries. Even when truce is declared, it is tenuous and rife with underlying tension. When we see Christian families we love and respect crumble, we know quite well that our home is not invincible.

There is a desperate need for a revival of "the hallowed circle of a family, thus united by love and sanctified by grace," and people are scrambling to find the silver bullet that will remedy the situation.

THROW ME A MAP

A young mother's letter to me expresses the heart cry of a generation of young parents.

> I feel so inadequate as a parent. My own mother was a self-absorbed alcoholic. She met many of my physical needs for food and clothing, but I was never nurtured. She certainly never taught me how to live as a godly woman. My father was an excellent provider, but he was seldom home. I worked so hard to please them both, hoping to achieve their love, but it never came. Now I am a thirty-six-year-old lost little girl who does not have a clue how to parent my own children. It's like trying to put a monster jigsaw puzzle together without the picture on the lid to guide me. It's not specific questions about parenting that I need answered as much as I need someone to show me how it's done. I know there isn't a formula or a list of easy answers, but surely someone who is farther down the parenting road than I am could at least shout directions or throw me a map.

My observation is that many young parents are befuddled about parenting because they have never been parented or, worse still, have been parented destructively. Many are from broken homes. Many are first-generation Christians who became believers through high school or college ministries. They were mothered by a generation of women who bought the feminist lie that mothering is unfulfilling and unimportant. It seems to me that there is a fragility and immaturity about this generation of parents that is a backwash of feminism. But I am greatly encouraged because they also have an intense desire to do it right. They are not looking for a quick fix. They are looking for the forgotten path. The path is forgotten because God is forgotten. "Because My people have forgotten Me, they have burned incense to worthless idols. And they have caused themselves to stumble in their ways, from the ancient paths, to walk in pathways and not on a highway" (Jeremiah 18:15 NKJV).

This young woman is asking the right question. "This is what the LORD says: 'Stand at the crossroads and look; ask for the ancient paths, ask where the good way is, and walk in it, and you will find rest for your souls'" (Jeremiah 6:16).

This young woman and her generation deserve an answer. It is part of their covenantal heritage. They do not need a one-size-fits-all solution. They do not need a behavioral policy manual. The covenant way is for one generation to "tell the next generation the praiseworthy deeds of the LORD, his power, and the wonders he has done. . . . so the next generation would know them, even the children yet to be born, and they in turn would tell their children. Then they would put their trust in God and would not forget his deeds but would keep his commands" (Psalm 78:4, 6-7).

This does not mean entitlement without responsibility. This young woman and her generation must be willing to listen and learn, and they must be willing to pay the price by persevering throughout the sanctifying process of seeking the mind of God and applying His truth to every situation. So this book is more about who God is than what we do. It is more about principle than performance. It is more about grace than guaranteed game plans.

We must move beyond behavior to belief. Family is really a theological issue because our families are products and expressions of our theology. We must have a biblical apologetic for family, or we will quickly drift from the ancient paths. These paths are not good just because they are old; they are good because they take us to God.

THE ANCIENT PATH

Here is the ancient path, the good way. Meditate on it and walk in it.

> *Great is the LORD and most worthy of praise; his greatness no one can fathom. One generation will commend your works to another; they will tell of your mighty acts. They will speak of the glorious splendor of your majesty, and I will meditate on your wonderful works. They will tell of the power of your awesome works. . . .*

> *They will tell of the glory of your kingdom and speak of your*
> *might, so that all men may know of your mighty acts and the glo-*
> *rious splendor of your kingdom. Your kingdom is an everlasting*
> *kingdom, and your dominion endures through all generations. The*
> *LORD is faithful to all his promises and loving toward all he has*
> *made.*
>
> PSALM 145:3-6, 11-13

The covenant way is for one generation to tell the next generation about the glorious splendor of God's kingdom.

For the last two or three decades, we have flocked to experts with
our questions about marriage and parenting. I am not discounting
their importance or their expertise, but perhaps we have neglected the
covenant way of listening to the previous generations. Older believers are farther down the path. They know things we need to know.

This exodus to the experts has not only robbed one generation
of hearing the wisdom of the next generation, but it has robbed the
older generation of the opportunity to share their life experiences.
And now many of the older generation lack the confidence to commend God's works to the next generation.

So in this book the next generation will tell us their stories. I have
asked some of my friends whom I have observed over several years
to tell us what they have learned about the Lord's faithfulness to all
His promises and His love toward His children. I am deeply grateful
to these friends for their gift to me and to those who read this book,
and I am sure that you will be grateful too. Each chapter opens with
a "Tell the Next Generation" story. The purpose is twofold—to tell
the younger generation of God's mighty acts and to equip the older
generation to continue commending God's works and ways to the
next generation. It's the covenant way.

AN EXPLANATION

This book stands alongside a previous book, *Heirs of the Covenant*. This
work is not a sequel. The two books actually go hand in hand, and it

does not matter which you read first. *Heirs* primarily pushes the doctrine of the covenant out into church life. This book focuses mainly on the home. But you really cannot separate the two. Both books are an attempt to think and live covenantally, so there are many repetitions and reinforcements. Each helps to clarify the other.

These books are better understood when studied with a group, and the endeavor will be even richer if it is a multi-generational/life season group. It is easier to do individual reading than group study, because it is easier to put the book down and walk away. Group study should result in mutual assistance, application, accountability, and affection—in a word, covenant.

Note: A leader's guide is available. Call: 800-283-1357.

MY PRAYER

Ancient Jewish wedding traditions were quite wonderful. On these most-celebrated social occasions virtually the whole village joined in the festivities.

Prior to the big event, the fathers of the bride and groom arranged the engagement. Then there was a betrothal ceremony where the couple exchanged vows in the presence of family and friends. Three kinds of gifts were given. The groom gave a gift to the bride's family. This gift sealed the betrothal covenant and bound the two families together. Second, there was a gift to the bride or groom from her father. Then there was the bridegroom's gift to the bride, usually clothes or jewelry.

After the betrothal ceremony, the groom returned home to prepare a place for his bride. Often this was an apartment in his father's house. She got ready for his return. She did not know exactly when he would come for her, but she knew that he would come because the betrothal covenant pledged him to do so.

When the bridegroom was ready, he left his father's house to claim his bride. His friends accompanied him on this journey, and as they wound through the village streets, others joined the joyful processional. The crowd grew larger, and the singing grew louder until it could be heard in the bride's home: "The bridegroom comes!"

The radiant bride met her bridegroom, and they went to his home for the wedding supper. Parents and friends blessed the couple, the couple made a covenant of faithfulness, and then they were escorted to the bridal chamber where the marriage was consummated.

Scripture is replete with references to Jesus as the heavenly Bridegroom and the church as His bride. He will come for His bride because He is bound by the betrothal covenant. He is a covenant keeper. He is preparing a place.

My prayer is that God will be pleased to use this book to help ready the bride for her Bridegroom.

> *As a bridegroom rejoices over his bride,*
> *so will your God rejoice over you.*
>
> ISAIAH 62:5

> *Let us be glad and rejoice and give Him glory,*
> *for the marriage of the Lamb has come,*
> *and His wife has made herself ready.*
>
> REVELATION 19:7 NKJV

PART ONE

The Covenant Way

If happiness is to be found upon earth,
it will be enjoyed within the hallowed circle of a family,
thus united by love and sanctified by grace.[1]

John Angell James

1

The Covenant Family

TELL THE NEXT GENERATION

Lynn Brookside, Escondido, California

Susan: *Lynn, I love the way you spiritually grandmother children even though you have no biological grandchildren. Tell us why you do this, and tell us some of the things you do for those children close by and for those who live far away.*

Lynn: *When I look into the face of a covenant child, I see the future of the church. I believe that my care for these young people contributes to the Christian heritage we will share with our descendants. I also want the children in my life to know that God loves them. The more intimately they know Him, the stronger and more stable their foundation—and that will help them to withstand our culture's gale force winds as they mature.*

Children love to get mail; it makes them feel important. So for children who don't live nearby, I send letters and jokes, as well as pictures that I've cut out of magazines. Once when some of my chosen grandchildren moved to a new town, I sent my "granddaughter" a picture of a hen with its chicks peeking out from under its wings. I wrote Psalm 91:4 under the picture and reminded her that God would be with her as she went to her new school the following week. To her younger brother, I sent a picture of a cloud formation that happened to look like a face in profile. I asked him whether he thought God made that cloud to remind us that He's always looking out for us, no matter where we live.

For little ones who live nearby, I plan special events such as Christmas cookie baking, making Mother's and Father's Day gifts for their parents, tea parties, and so forth. And while we bake, do crafts, or have tea, we talk about Jesus and His love for us.

I also phone my chosen grandchildren periodically. I make sure to talk only to the child for whom I've called and no one else in the family. That way the child knows that I phoned specifically to talk with him or her. I can talk with the parents at another time.

These things create a storehouse of special memories that enrich our lives—theirs and mine.

The family home is the nursery of love.
Intimacy grows where we live together. But in Scripture the home
is always only a means to an end, the medium by which
we begin to understand the relationship
we have together with God.[1]

ABRAHAM KUYPER

I want to live in Mitford. If you are one of the millions who have read Jan Karon's wildly successful books, you may also want to buy a house next door to Father Tim and Cynthia. These tales of a warm-hearted community of wacky and wonderful people have definitely touched a nerve. The Mitford phenomenon is intriguing because we live in a culture of isolation, privatization, and cyberspace virtual relationships—yet these books are being gobbled up by people who want what they describe. Mitford is a place where the church is the center of community life and people assume their responsibility for one another. I think Jan Karon has captured the essence of covenant life, and people are lining up to vicariously live in that place.

In later chapters we will look specifically at marriage and parenting, but in this chapter we will consider the context in which Christian marriage and parenting are to exist—the covenant family, the family of families, the church. It is imperative that we understand this context because our notions about family are usually shaped more by culture than by Scripture, and we live in a culture of individualism, selfism, and materialism—all of which are hostile to cultivating an environment of grace in our homes.

This hostility has been exacerbated by the untruth of evolution. Evolutionists explain family as a human invention based on expediency. When family is built on an evolutionary psychology, the logical conclusion is a power grab, a survival of the fittest. Self-interest stakes out its own territory and then proceeds to seize control of surrounding territories as well.

Add to this mix baby boomers' distrust of established institutions such as government, schools, and churches, and the misery and confusion in families is not surprising. What is surprising is that there is not even more dysfunction. An article in *Christianity Today* said that baby boomers have "turned this distrust into a social norm. . . . As a consequence, [they] have reoriented our society toward peers and away from family. They have moved the psychic center of the family away from obligations to others and toward self-fulfillment. They have raised to new ideological heights the ideal of individual autonomy fused with democratic egalitarianism."[2]

This distortion seeps into many Christian families in the form of family individualism. The nuclear family becomes an island unto itself. Members are devoted to one another but detached from the covenant family. The motive is noble—there is an intense desire to protect. But the strategy is flawed—they isolate and barricade.

We need to recapture the glorious principle of covenant living. It may be shocking to consider the implications of the covenant in crafting our families, but in the covenant we find the right way.

WHAT DOES THE COVENANT WAY LOOK LIKE?

My friend Pam Benton, a pastor's wife in St. Louis, describes it well.

> *Family.* There has never been a time in my life when that word and all the people encompassed by the word have not been a major part of who I am. I have always known who I am because of who I have been related to. My place in a family has identified me, even to myself.
>
> My daddy died when I was two, but my strong, sweet relationship with my mother and a large extended family protected me from fear—even from the feeling of being orphaned. I was loved, protected, taught, encouraged, corrected, and cared for by my family. At some point in my

early life I began to understand that my sisters and I were safe not just because of a dozen loving uncles, but because there was another Father, a heavenly Father, who would never die. He would never leave me or fail me if I was His. I learned that God is real and that He loves me. I never questioned that.

The day came when even as a child I began to understand that the family that loved and cared for us was larger than aunts, uncles, grandparents, and cousins. It was a church full of people. It was God's family. This larger part of my family began to teach me new things about my heavenly Father and about my responsibilities in the family.

The day came when I learned that this was not just the story of my life. After I asked Jesus into my heart, or rather when He invited me into His heart, I learned that this wonderful family life was God's plan for all His children, that He puts us into families for many reasons.

It is in this family of God that I have been taught to know and to love His Word, that I have been shown by example how to live according to His Word, that I have been encouraged to study it and memorize it. It is in this family of God that I have been corrected and that I have been held accountable by the loving concern and the support of family members.

It is in this family of God that I have been comforted when frightened or in pain and enfolded during hard times. I have experienced loyalty that I certainly do not deserve because I have been loved in the family for the Father's sake.

It is in this family of God that I have been served in my times of need and that I have been given the privilege of serving others in their need. I have been constantly reminded to love the individuals in my family because that is the way God has chosen for me to show my love for Him.

It is in the safety of this family of God that windows have been opened for me, that I have been shown a lost and dying world, and that I have been challenged and equipped to move into that world with the Good News of the Gospel.

This family has been God's very arms about me all of my life. I cannot conceive of life without it. It has been the constant, visible reality of God's love for me over and over again

I can almost hear some of you shouting, "But I am separated spiritually and/or geographically from my family. I don't have what Pam had." Read on. My husband's testimony is very different than Pam's but just as covenantal. Gene's testimony used to make me sad because I did not like to think of him growing up in a non-Christian home. Now I love to hear Gene tell his story because I understand that it is the story of the obedience of God's family.

My life is a picture of God's sovereign grace. I was born into a non-Christian family where there was never the slightest effort to even appear religious. I don't recall my parents ever taking me to church. The only time God was mentioned in our home was when my mother and dad argued. I was an unlikely candidate to become a Christian. Yet God in His mercy reached into this situation and found me. The doctrine of God's sovereign election has never been a problem for me. I am a living illustration of this wonder.

When my dad died, we moved back to my mother's hometown. I look back and see clearly that it was God's providence that put us in a neighborhood where there was a little Presbyterian church willing to reach out to a young boy whose life could have gone in any direction. Sonny was my boyhood friend. His mother was the organist and choir director, so when the church doors opened, she was there. Sonny had no evangelistic fervor, and I had no consuming desire to know about God. Sonny just didn't want to go to church alone, so he would drag me along.

I spent a lot of time at the church and was exposed to a lot of preaching and teaching. It's interesting to me that I do not remember specific sermons or Sunday school lessons. I remember the warmth and love of a church family. I remember picnics and rousing singing. The church kids were my best friends. Many of their parents were our youth leaders. They opened their hearts and homes to me and accepted me as a part of their covenant family. I was in and out of their homes regularly. Families like the Harrisons and the Fullers and the Holts showed me what Christian families look like. I was enfolded into this community of believers and moved among them as if I belonged. It never occurred to me that I was an outsider. It all seemed perfectly natural and normal. Now I see that it was supernatural. It was the Gospel of grace being lived out in daily life.

Gradually I came to see my need for a Savior and committed my life to Jesus. I was a teenager when I began to feel that I was being called into the gospel ministry. My church family rejoiced with me, but they did not seem surprised. They acted as if they had expected it all along. When I look back, I'm amazed that they never resented the little boy who tagged along with one of their own and who had no resources to contribute to the church. Now I understand that they invested in me because that's the covenant way.

I'm thankful that our children have very different childhood memories and that our grandchildren are growing up in Christian homes, but I do not regret my past. "The boundary lines have fallen for me in pleasant places; surely I have a delightful inheritance. I will praise the LORD, who counsels me. . . . I have set the LORD always before me. Because he is at my right hand, I will not be shaken. Therefore my heart is glad and my tongue rejoices. . . . You have made known to me the path of life; you will fill me with joy in your presence, with eternal pleasures at your right hand" (Psalm 16:6-9, 11).

WHAT, WHY, AND HOW

The covenant of grace is what we believe, but the nature of the covenant must also determine what we do, why we do it, and how we do it. Perhaps this is where we have failed to speak with clarity.

Even in churches and families where the theology is precise, too often the methodology for building families is a composite. Churches and families grab the latest how-to book on marriage or parenting. We assume that if it works, it must be right, regardless of the underlying theology. We look at the temporary product rather than the truth of God's Word. And yet we make a dangerous dichotomy when we separate right doctrine from righteous living. To disconnect behavior from belief robs the behavior of vitality, integrity, and longevity.

When we return to the ancient paths, we are reminded that the family exists within the sphere of the covenant. Individual households are to join hands with others in the community of faith and declare their interdependence.

Chapter 3 will give more explanation about the covenant, but for now we will think about the ambiance of covenant life in the covenant community by analyzing and applying various characteristics of the covenant. Before we do that, let me emphasize that family may mean a husband and wife and children, or it may mean a single parent, or grandparents, or a single person. Whatever the configuration, if the person or persons are Christian, this family exists within the realm of the covenant.

CHARACTERISTICS OF THE COVENANT

In *Heirs of the Covenant* I discussed several characteristics of the covenant that can help us think and live covenantally (pages 30-33). Here I will make application of these to the family.

The covenant is relational. The God of heaven and earth is a personal God who establishes an intimate covenant relationship with His people. He binds Himself to us in covenant faithfulness. Our relationships with each other are to mirror His relationship with us. This is a relational model built on doctrines such as justification and adoption. God declares us to be just in His sight on the basis of the merits of Christ. He adopts us as His children and accepts us into His family, not because of our performance but because of His grace. These are the reasons we accept and love one another. Our relationships in the family are not about living up to each other's expectations. They are about accepting one another and reflecting God's grace to each other as we are being transformed by the power of the Gospel.

The covenant is sovereignly initiated. The more we understand this divine initiative, the more we understand that we deserve nothing but have been given everything. This knowledge produces a humility that frees us to "Do nothing out of selfish ambition or vain conceit, but in humility consider others better than yourselves. Each of you should look not only to your own interests, but also to the interests of others" (Philippians 2:3-4). This describes a haven of grace.

The covenant is sovereignly sustained and thus eternally secure. The confidence that one can "cast your cares on the LORD and he will sustain you; he will never let the righteous fall" (Psalm 55:22) gives security and peace to a home.

The covenant is Trinitarian. The unity of the Trinity is evidenced in the work of creation and redemption. This oneness of purpose is to be reflected in marriage. The unity/diversity principle is also to be evident in the covenant community.

The covenant is corporate. Salvation is personal, but God does not deal with us just as individuals. He adopts us into His family. He deals with us as His children. We are a household of faith, a covenant community. These relationships are not just a matter of personal taste, choice, or our good judgment in choosing one another. These relationships are sovereignly designed.

The covenant is generational. Throughout Scripture there is the emphasis that one generation is to tell the next generation the praiseworthy deeds of the Lord and the wonders He has done. We find repeated commands to parents and to the covenant community to teach and nurture the children.

The covenant is compassionate. God is a God of compassion, and His people are to be people of compassion. We must teach our children and grandchildren how to love and care for others because this is an expression of our theology. It's the covenant way. It's Christ's way.

The covenant is integrative. The covenant is the thread that holds

Scripture together. This gives us an all-encompassing worldview, an integrated framework to think about God's truth and to apply that truth in all of life. It unshackles us from the tendency to aim for behavioral change apart from grace. A covenantal approach gives secure boundaries within which there is room for creative flexibility.

The covenant is exclusive. "You shall have no other gods before me. You shall not make for yourself an idol. . . . You shall not bow down to them or worship them; for I, the LORD your God, am a jealous God . . ." (Exodus 20:3-5). Neither we nor our children can serve two masters (Matthew 6:24). We must be vigilant in guarding our children against the cultural idols of our day.

The covenant is inclusive. We are commissioned to "go into all the world and preach the good news to all creation" (Mark 16:15). Our homes should be outward focused. They should not only be places of grace for our family, but our hearts and doors should be open to welcome others.

The deeper our roots go into biblical truth, the more stable our family tree. So stay with me as we add another characteristic of the covenant that is especially applicable to this book.

THE COVENANT IS FAMILIAL

From the beginning God worked through families. He established marriage, and He commanded Adam and Eve to be fruitful and multiply. After the Fall, the covenant promise had to do with their seed. It was through their offspring that God would keep the promise of salvation.

Then in Genesis 12 we read: "The LORD had said to Abram, 'Leave your country, your people and your father's household and go to the land I will show you. I will make you into a great nation and I will bless you'" (Genesis 12:1-2).

When God revealed Himself to Abram as the Lord, the personal God of covenant faithfulness, He bound Himself to Abram, and the promise extended to Abram's offspring. Later God appeared to Abram again and made it even clearer that the covenant is familial.

"Abram fell facedown, and God said to him, '. . . No longer will you be called Abram; your name will be Abraham, for I have made you a father of many nations. I will make you very fruitful; I will make nations of you, and kings will come from you. I will establish my covenant as an everlasting covenant between me and you and your descendants after you for the generations to come, to be your God and the God of your descendants after you'" (Genesis 17:3, 5-7).

Then God gave the covenant sign. "'You are to undergo circumcision, and it will be the sign of the covenant between me and you. For the generations to come every male among you who is eight days old must be circumcised. . . . My covenant in your flesh is to be an everlasting covenant. Any uncircumcised male, who has not been circumcised in the flesh, will be cut off from his people; he has broken my covenant'" (Genesis 17:11-14).

This sign further solidified the familial nature of the covenant. *The New Geneva Study Bible* explains:

> By this ritual the organ of procreation was consecrated to God. . . . Some ancient Near Eastern cultures circumcised their children at puberty as a rite of passage from childhood to manhood. God employed the sign for infants to show that the children of believing parents are "holy"—they are separated from the profane world and belong to the covenant community (Rom. 11:16; 1 Cor. 7:14). God continues to use the family institution (Acts 16:31). The initiation rite into the covenant community today is baptism. In Christ there is no longer male or female, Jew or Gentile, so all may come (Gal. 3:26-29; Col. 2:11, 12). . . . The covenant promises were extended to all within the household of faith. Even in the Old Testament, the scope of the covenant community was not exclusively determined by ancestry—foreshadowing the expansion of the covenant to a multitude from every tribe and nation.[3]

Charles Hodge, a nineteenth-century Princeton Theological Seminary professor and renowned theologian, wrote:

In the sight of God parents and children are one. The former are the authorized representatives of the latter; they act for them; they contract obligations in their name. In all cases, therefore, where parents enter into covenant with God, they bring their children with them. . . . If a man joined the commonwealth of Israel, he secured for his children the benefits of the theocracy, unless they willingly renounced them. And so when a believer adopts the covenant of grace, he brings his children within that covenant, in the sense that God promises to give them, in his own good time, all the benefits of redemption, provided they do not willingly renounce their baptismal engagements.[4]

The genealogies of the Old Testament sometimes seem laborious. We wonder why God would take up space rehearsing over and over who begat whom. Does it really matter? The answer is a resounding *YES*. Families matter. In some mysterious way, God works through families. The opening words of the New Testament highlight this. When the fullness of time came, and God sent forth His Son into the world, rather than jumping to the good stuff about the angels and the light and the glory, God once again painstakingly reiterates the genealogy. It is as if He is shouting to us that the covenant thread runs through families.

Abraham, his son Isaac, and his grandson Jacob were the patriarchs of this covenant family. Jacob's twelve sons emigrated to Egypt. They were a prolific bunch, and eventually the pharaoh enslaved them. Then God sent Moses to rescue them.

FROM A FAMILY TO A KINGDOM

Three months after Moses led the Israelites out of Egypt, they arrived at Sinai.

Then Moses went up to God, and the LORD called to him from the mountain and said, "This is what you are . . . to tell the people of Israel: 'You yourselves have seen what I did to Egypt, and

*how I carried you on eagles' wings and brought you to myself. Now
if you obey me fully and keep my covenant, then out of all nations
you will be my treasured possession. Although the whole earth is
mine, you will be for me a kingdom of priests and a holy nation."*

EXODUS 19:3-6

Here we see the transition from a family to "a kingdom of priests
and a holy nation." Now the familial and corporate characteristics of
the covenant merge.

As God gives the people a covenant document that explains how
they are to live in covenant with Him, He begins by reminding them
of His relationship with them. In the divine initiative—"I brought you
to myself"—we see that the covenant relationship precedes the
covenant requirements: grace before law. The covenant terms—"if you
obey me fully and keep my covenant"—were possible because first
God brought the Israelites to Himself and bound Himself to them.

Then God gave the Ten Commandments. The sights and sounds
were awesome. The mountain shook, and so did the people. They
stood at a distance, but "Moses approached the thick darkness where
God was" (Exodus 20:21). When Moses went back down the mountain, he was shocked to find the people worshiping a golden calf. This
is a decisive moment for the fledgling nation.

The Lord struck them with a plague, and then He said to Moses:

*Leave this place, you and the people you brought up out of Egypt,
and go up to the land I promised on oath to Abraham, Isaac and
Jacob, saying, "I will give it to your descendants." I will send an
angel before you and drive out the Canaanites, Amorites, Hittites,
Perizzites, Hivites and Jebusites. Go up to the land flowing with
milk and honey. But I will not go with you, because you are a stiff-
necked people and I might destroy you on the way.*

EXODUS 33:1-3

The people were stiff-necked, but at least they understood that
even an angel assigned to drive out their enemies so that they could

possess the land was not sufficient. The withdrawal of God's presence obliterated any benefits of angelic assistance or acquisition of valuable real estate. "When the people heard these distressing words, they began to mourn" (Exodus 33:4).

Then before we find out what happens next, there is a brief interlude when Moses gives us a revealing piece of information: "Now Moses used to take a tent and pitch it outside the camp some distance away, calling it the 'tent of meeting.' Anyone inquiring of the LORD would go to the tent of meeting outside the camp" (Exodus 33:7). Very interesting. The tent of meeting, the place that represented God's presence among His people, was located *outside* the camp.

Now back to the crisis at hand. "Moses said to the LORD. . . . 'Remember that this nation is your people'" (Exodus 33:12-13). Moses, the mediator of the old covenant whose ministry foreshadows that of the Mediator of the new covenant, stood between God and the people. He did what the greater Moses would do in a greater way. He knew He could not ask God to go with them on the basis of the people's performance. Their hope was in God's promise to be their God and to live among them. Their hope was in God's grace and mercy.

God's reply reveals the essence of the covenant promise: "The LORD replied, 'My Presence will go with you, and I will give you rest'" (Exodus 33:14).

Moses' response reveals the distinctive nature of God's covenant people: "Then Moses said to him, 'If your Presence does not go with us, do not send us up from here. How will anyone know that you are pleased with me and with your people unless you go with us? What else will distinguish me and your people from all the other people on the face of the earth?'" (Exodus 33:15-16).

God's presence brings rest to our souls and rest in our homes. God's presence will distinguish us and our family from all the other families on the planet. God's presence will empower us to reflect His goodness to one another. This is intimately personal, but it is not individualistic. Notice Moses' use of singular and plural pronouns: "'O LORD, if I have found favor in your eyes,' he said, 'then let the LORD go with us. Although this is a stiff-necked people, forgive our wickedness and our sin, and take us as your inheritance'" (Exodus 34:9).

God's promise to Moses is His promise to us: "Then the LORD said: 'I am making a covenant with you. Before all your people I will do wonders never before done in any nation in all the world. The people you live among will see how awesome is the work that I, the LORD, will do for you'" (Exodus 34:10).

Then God gave Moses detailed examples of how the Ten Words of the Covenant should be applied to all areas of life in the covenant community. Much of this instruction had to do with worship. There were precise directions for building the tabernacle. Moses returned with this blueprint, the people followed every detail, and when the work was completed, "the cloud covered the Tent of Meeting, and the glory of the LORD filled the tabernacle" (Exodus 40:34).

This stunning picture is an object lesson for God's people on this side of the cross. John's Gospel tells us that "the Word became flesh and made his dwelling among us. We have seen his glory, the glory of the One and Only, who came from the Father, full of grace and truth" (John 1:14). Because Jesus *tabernacled* among us and accomplished the work of redemption, the glorious reality is that He now resides in us. "Do you not know that your body is a temple of the Holy Spirit, who is in you, whom you have received from God?" (1 Corinthians 6:19).

Nothing about the Old Testament tabernacle was left to human invention, including the placement of this visible representation of God's presence among them. "The LORD said to Moses and Aaron: 'The Israelites are to camp around the Tent of Meeting some distance from it, each man under his standard with the banners of his family'" (Numbers 2:1-2).

No longer would the tabernacle be outside the camp. It would be smack-dab in the middle. It had to be. If stiff-necked people keep God's presence at a distance, they will become more selfish, rebellious, and isolated. They will echo Cain's defiance, "Am I my brother's keeper?" (Genesis 4:9). If any Israelite family had packed up their tent and traveled through the desert alone, they would have been vulnerable and defenseless; but even worse, they would have separated themselves from God's glory.

This fact, too, has very practical application for God's covenant people today. This is what Jesus prayed for us: "I have given them the glory that you gave me, that they may be one as we are one: I in them and you in me. May they be brought to complete unity to let the world know that you sent me and have loved them even as you have loved me" (John 17:22-23).

Jesus shows us His glory so that we may be one. When we remember His terms of endearment for His church, this should not surprise us. He speaks of us as His body (Ephesians 1:23) and His family (Ephesians 2:19). To separate from His body is to separate from Him. Community solidarity strengthens and protects each individual family and equips families to build homes that are little sanctuaries of grace because our oneness draws us closer to His glory.

For Gene and me, our zeal to understand this concept has been rekindled with the gift of grandchildren. Our desire to tell the next generation the praiseworthy deeds of the Lord and for them to understand the wonder of being a part of God's family has made us take a second look at the familial and corporate nature of the covenant. But it was the death of a grandchild that plunged us into the comfort of living within the sphere of the covenant.

A LEGACY OF GRACE

A tradition in our family is that children are named for someone in the family. When our daughter Kathryn and her husband, Dean, were expecting their fifth child, they told their other children her name would be Annie Grace. My middle name is Ann, but the children could not understand why they would name a baby Grace. "No one in our family has that name," they said. Kathryn and Dean responded, "We are saved by grace, we live by grace, and we are in God's family because of His grace. It really is a family name." The children's confusion was assuaged. Our family prayer was that Annie Grace's life would be a celebration of God's glorious grace and that she would always rest in the sufficiency of His grace.

A few days after Annie's birth we learned that she had a hole in her heart. When she was eleven weeks old, she had surgery. Her little heart was weaker than the doctors thought, and she died a few hours after the surgery.

Gene and I love John Bunyan's *Pilgrim's Progress*. One of our favorite scenes from that book is when Christian and Hopeful cross the river to the Celestial City. Christian begins to sink, and Hopeful cries out, "Be of good cheer. I feel the bottom, and it is good."[5] When Annie died, our hearts were shattered, but we can still shout with hopeful voices, "We felt the Rock, and He is good."

We can also adapt Bunyan's line and say, "Be of good cheer, fellow pilgrims. We saw the covenant community at work, and it is good." Human language is inadequate to describe the wonder and beauty of God's people living out the reality of their relationship with Him. This is a feeble attempt to describe that marvelous phenomenon.

Kathryn and Dean are members of Decatur Presbyterian Church in Decatur, Alabama. Several people from the church were with us at the hospital during the surgery, but when we received word that Annie was not doing well, the waiting room was soon filled with people. When the doctor told Kathryn and Dean that Annie would only live a little longer and that they could go into intensive care and stay with her, I saw horror on Kathryn's face. "I can't watch her die," she cried as they walked into ICU. Immediately the church in the waiting room began to pray that God would give them grace to parent Annie to the gates of heaven. When the nurse took Gene and me to Annie's bedside, we saw the incredible answer to those prayers.

Dean was sitting in a rocking chair, Kathryn was in his lap, and they were holding Annie. I have never seen such extraordinary peace. They rocked Annie, talked to her about heaven, and told her how much they loved her. They told her that she would soon be worshiping Jesus face to face.

After a while we reminded them that the church was in the waiting room and asked if they would like for the people gathered to tell

Annie good-bye. Kathryn and Dean could have clutched for themselves those last moments with Annie, but they acted covenantally. The covenant family began coming in two or three at a time. They kissed Annie. They wept. When Annie began worshiping God face to face, we joined the church in the waiting room and worshiped Him together.

Over the next days, weeks, and months this covenant community continued to surround this family with tender love. They did not just weep *for* Kathryn and Dean; they wept *with* them. They believed that Annie had been entrusted to their church family, and they loved her. They did not stand at a distance and watch. They entered into her living and her dying, and they continue to care for her parents and siblings in remarkable ways. When the other children asked why people were doing so many things for them, Kathryn and Dean would reply, "This is the body of Christ taking care of us." At one point I was flooded with fear wondering about the effect of Annie's death on her precious brothers and sisters. But I quickly realized that they were not learning about death in a vacuum. They were experiencing this reality in the context of a community of love.

This congregation is faithfully taught about God's grace, and they faithfully cultivate an environment of grace. Carol Godwin, the wife of an elder in this church, wrote these words as a gift to Kathryn and Dean and their children. This tribute is framed and now hangs in their home.

> *God sent us a little girl*
> *Who changed us forever.*
> *He showed us how to love, to suffer, and*
> *To cling to Him through a tiny child that*
> *Never said a word, but whose life spoke*
> *More loudly than a thousand voices.*
> *May His words sink into the depths of our*
> *Souls and cause us to be more like Him.*
> *We praise You, Lord, for teaching us*
> *Through Your Grace.*

Another tender example of the strength of covenant life was the ability that Kathryn and Dean had to make good decisions during a time of such intense pain. They planned a funeral that would help their children, family, and friends, as well as a watching community, fix their eyes on Jesus. First we went to the cemetery and buried Annie. Then we went to the church and worshiped. The first hymn expressed the message Kathryn and Dean wanted everyone to know.

All praise to God, who reigns above, The God of all creation,
The God of wonders, pow'r and love, The God of our salvation!
With healing balm my soul He fills, The God who ev'ry sorrow stills,
To God all praise and glory!

What God's almighty pow'r hath made His gracious mercy keepeth;
By morning dawn or evening shade His watchful eye ne'er sleepeth;
Within the kingdom of His might, Lo, all is just and all is right,
To God all praise and glory!

I cried to Him in time of need; Lord God, O, hear my calling!
For death He gave me life indeed And kept my feet from falling.
For this my thanks shall endless be;
*   O, thank Him, thank our God, with me,*
To God all praise and glory!

The Lord forsaketh not His flock, His chosen generation;
He is their Refuge and their Rock, Their Peace and their Salvation.
As with a mother's tender hand He leads His own, His chosen band,
To God all praise and glory!

Ye who confess Christ's holy Name, To God give praise and glory!
Ye who the Father's pow'r proclaim, To God give praise and glory!
All idols under foot be trod, The Lord is God. The Lord is God!
To God all praise and glory!

Then come before His presence now And banish fear and sadness;
To your Redeemer pay your vow and sing with joy and gladness;

> *Though great distress my soul befell,*
> *The Lord, my God did all things well,*
> *To God all praise and glory!*[6]

Later I had a glimpse into the source of this strength. Our other daughter Laurin told me that she had asked the Lord to let her carry some of Kathryn's pain, at least through the funeral. Laurin did suffer intense grief, and her sister seemed to be in a bubble of grace. Laurin obeyed the command to "carry each other's burdens, and in this way you will fulfill the law of Christ" (Galatians 6:2).

The covenant community is part of our inheritance. It is in this community that the cords of the covenant hold us when we are weak and vulnerable. The defining characteristic of this community is God's presence among us. Our unity validates that reality.

THE CORDS OF THE COVENANT

In her beautiful book *Holiness in Hidden Places,* Joni Eareckson Tada gives a breathtaking example of the cords of the covenant. She writes about the sacrament of Communion, a sign and seal of the covenant of grace, the family supper when God's children gather around His table to remember.

Yesterday was a day to remember. It was the day to celebrate communion—at least in my church. So literally, it was a day of remembrance. It's curious that God didn't command any sacrament to commemorate His birth, life, miracles, or resurrection. Only His death.

For me, the Lord's Supper is always a powerful visual symbol. Maybe it's because we actually handle the bread and lift the wine to our lips. Yet as the plate of crackers is passed, we're ever so careful to lift our little "pinkie" and aim for our cracker without touching any of the others. Our fastidious care, although tidy, also seems symbolic: we go to such extraordinary efforts to live our lives totally isolated from each other, even though we are *one* in Christ.

. . . my friend sitting next to me reached into the plate to get crackers for both of us. Then, after the pastor invited us all to participate, she lifted one piece to my mouth and then the other piece to hers. I can't take communion by myself. . . . I'm forced to depend on another Christian to handle my bread for me.

I'm glad about that. It makes me feel connected. Interdependent. One with others. It's a happy symbol of how closely I must live my life with fellow believers. I can't live my life alone and isolated.

Communion celebrates the body of Christ, broken on the cross. Communion celebrates the Body of Christ, the Church. Communion is a celebration of unity.

Oh, how I wish we'd remember important things like this when the bread and wine are passed.[7]

THE ANCIENT PATH

Here is the ancient path, the good way. Meditate on it and make this your prayer for your church family.

> *My purpose is that they may be encouraged in heart and united in love, so that they may have the full riches of complete understanding, in order that they may know the mystery of God, namely, Christ, in whom are hidden all the treasures of wisdom and knowledge.*

COLOSSIANS 2:2-3

QUESTIONS AND ANSWERS

Q. What do we do? Where do we start?

A. Good question. We will unfold the answer as we proceed through this book. But for now, be encouraged. You have every resource you need to make your home a place of grace. God has given you His Word, His Holy Spirit, the privilege of prayer, and the church. Start here. For example:

• A daily personal devotional time is indispensable. Read God's Word and pray. This is how we fix our eyes on Jesus. If this is new for you, begin by reading, rereading, mediating on, and praying through the Scriptures listed in the Bible study at the end of each chapter in this book. Then you may want to use a plan that takes you through the Scriptures in a year. Pray that the Holy Spirit will give you wisdom to apply them in your life and your family's life. Scripture is God's revelation of Himself. We fix our eyes on Jesus by looking at Him as He shows us Himself in His Word.

• Family devotions are essential for homes to be places of grace. Determine a time when your family can gather each day for ten or fifteen minutes. Read a portion of Scripture or an age-appropriate Bible storybook, memorize Bible verses, sing a hymn, pray together. Select a portion of Scripture and pray this every day for your children. For example, pray Proverbs 3:5-7 as you ask the Lord to enable you and your children to trust Him with all your hearts and never lean on your own understanding. Pray that you will acknowledge Him in everything—that you will submit to His authority in all of life.

• Whether you are a single or a family with several people, evaluate your relationship to the church.

How does your family prepare for worship? You may want to read sections from Psalm 119, or read Psalm 100, to prepare your hearts. Spend time praying for the pastor, Sunday school teachers, and other worshipers.

Do you keep church at a distance, or is your family vitally connected to your church family?

Do you think more about what the church does for you or about how you can serve the church?

Do you open your heart and home to members of the church family? The grace of hospitality knits hearts together.

Do you pray faithfully for the leaders in your church and for those with special needs?

Do you weep with those who weep and rejoice with those who rejoice in very practical ways? Take a meal to new parents and celebrate the gift of their child with them. Visit a shut-in. Invite a single for lunch. Do chores for an elderly member of your church. Babysit for a single parent. Write a note to a couple recently bereaved by miscarriage.

Q. What application does this have to the church?

A. The church should be intentional in teaching the content of the covenant in the context of covenant relationships that validate the Gospel of grace. This is discussed in detail in *Heirs of the Covenant.*

BIBLE STUDY

1. Read Exodus 33.
   - Why did the people mourn (verses 3 and 4)? *because God would not go in their midst*
   - What does God promise in verse 14? *His presence will go w/them & give them rest.*
   - Read Matthew 11:28-30.
   - According to Exodus 33:15-16, what is the distinguishing characteristic of the people of God? *Gods presence with them*
   - Read Matthew 28:18-20.

2. Read the following and list things you learn about the church.
   Matthew 16:18 *the church is built on Christ, the Son of God*
   Acts 14:23, 27 *appointed elders for every church, told all God had done*
   Acts 20:28 *Overseers to be on guard, shepherd the church*
   Ephesians 1:22-23 *all things in subjection to Christ; He is head of Church which is His body*
   Ephesians 5:23-32 *Christ head of Church & Savior of body Christ loved church & gave Himself up for her. Sanctifies her, presents her.*
   Colossians 1:13-24 *Christ is the head of the body*
   1 Timothy 3:14-15 *Church of living God is pillar & support of the truth.*

3. Read the following and make a list of our covenant responsibilities to one another.
   Romans 12:10, 13-18 *devoted, giving preference to one another, contribute to needs, practice hospitality, be at peace*
   Romans 14:13, 19 *don't judge & don't be a stumbling block. Pursue things that make for peace, build up one another*
   Romans 15:5-7 *be of same mind w/one voice glorify God. Accept one another*
   Ephesians 4:2-3, 32 *& diligent to preserve unity of spirit in bond of peace, kind to one another, tender hearted, forgiving one another.*

Ephesians 5:21
1 Thessalonians 5:11-15
Hebrews 3:13
Hebrews 10:24-25
James 4:11
James 5:9, 16, 19-20
1 Peter 4:8-10

2

Three Homes

TELL THE NEXT GENERATION

Wilson and Pam Benton, St. Louis, Missouri

Susan: *Wilson and Pam, over the years I have watched you blend your home and church life into a beautiful, harmonious piece. Tell us why and how you did that.*

Wilson and Pam: *We always knew that God's call to serve Him was to us as a couple. As He brought children into our family, we believed that His call to serve included them as well. We committed ourselves to pray that they would love our way of life as a "ministry family" and never resent being "preacher's kids."*

Rather than resenting that they were often the only children at the midweek prayer service, they hurried to their spot on the back row with an adopted grandmother or aunt, always feeling very grown-up and important as they shared their own prayer requests with the group. Giving up their bedrooms for the visiting preacher or missionary became an event anticipated with great excitement because they assumed that these special people were coming just to see them. They never complained that we didn't have enough "family time" because the church family was family to them. They could hardly imagine Sunday lunch, Thanksgiving, Christmas, Easter, or even a rare free evening not including part of that extended family, often at their insistence. After praying for a sick friend around our table for months, it seemed only right to them for Wilson to cancel a long-awaited family camping trip when that special friend died. Giving up their daddy was their contribution to the bereaved family.

There were times when we would have shielded them from conflicts and problems in our church, but as they got older, this became impossible. And besides, when they watched us face hard times, they learned to deal with criticism, disappointment, schism, and other assorted occupational hazards. Our gracious God used these difficult times to help them grow and to make them feel essential in our family's calling.

God also equipped the three of them to minister to us when our hearts were hurting or our faith failing. During one period of intense criticism Pam was almost paralyzed with fear. Returning home one day, we discovered that Louis, Paige, and Laura had plastered the walls of our house with posters hand-printed with Scripture verses reminding her of God's promises! How thankful we were that in grace we had been kept from separating our home life from our ministry. As Paige informed the pulpit search committee in St. Louis: "The Bentons are a package deal." And we still are! Even today our children's lives provide our greatest credibility for ministry.

Let me exhort all governors of families,
in the name of our Lord Jesus Christ, often to reflect
on the inestimable worth of their own souls and the infinite ransom,
even the precious blood of Jesus Christ, which has been paid down for them
. . . and you will no more neglect your family's spiritual welfare
than your own.[1]

GEORGE WHITEFIELD

*I*n this chapter we will look to the past, to the future, and to the present. The first home and our future home give us glorious glimpses of God and of His design for family. We will consider the implications of what we learn about these homes as we think about the third home—my home and your home.

THE GARDEN HOME

The Garden Home was a place of grace. After calling creation into existence, the triune God created man and woman in His own image. God said, "Let us make man in our image, in our likeness . . ." (Genesis 1:26). "The LORD God formed the man from the dust of the ground and breathed into his nostrils the breath of life, and the man became a living being" (Genesis 2:7).

Because the man was created in God's image, he had the capacity to live in fellowship with God. Man could live face to face with God and then turn and reflect the glory of God to others. God gave the man the almost-perfect home. "Now the LORD God had planted a garden in the east, in Eden; and there he put the man he had formed" (v. 8).

After every act of creation God spoke a benediction: "It is good." Now for the first time God spoke a malediction: "It is not good for the man to be alone" (v. 18). This was not a divine blunder. It was the divine blueprint. Man's aloneness was not good because God designed him to live in companionship. So God said, "I will make a helper suitable for him" (v. 18).

This was not just good. God pronounced it *very* good.

Now the almost-perfect home was perfect because there was someone to whom and with whom man could reflect God's glory. It is no wonder that Adam's joy exploded in a passionate love poem that captures the essence of God's plan for family: "This is now bone of my bones and flesh of my flesh; she shall be called 'woman,' for she was taken out of man. For this reason a man will leave his father and mother and be united to his wife, and they will become one flesh" (vv. 23-24). The result is not surprising: "The man and his wife were both naked, and they felt no shame" (v. 25).

They were given a cultural mandate: "God blessed them and said to them, 'Be fruitful and increase in number; fill the earth and subdue it. Rule over the fish of the sea and the birds of the air and over every living creature that moves on the ground'" (Genesis 1:28).

And God provided the king and queen of the garden the necessary resources to fulfill their responsibilities: "God said, 'I give you every seed-bearing plant on the face of the whole earth and every tree that has fruit with seed in it. They will be yours for food. And to all the beasts of the earth and all the birds of the air and all the creatures that move on the ground—everything that has the breath of life in it—I give every green plant for food'" (vv. 29-30).

GARDEN-VARIETY PRINCIPLES

We can learn some foundational truths from the Garden Home.

The Lord God formed man, and the Lord God put him in the garden. The combination of these two names for God is significant. "God" reveals Him as the sovereign Creator. "Lord" is His personal name and shows His personal relationship with and commitment to the man and woman.

God built the Garden Home. This sanctuary was fashioned and furnished by God. It was His gift to His creatures. It was the place where they belonged.

The man and woman were created in God's image. They had the capacity to live in intimate fellowship with God and to represent Him to one another. There was equality of status as God's image-bearers.

They were created male and female. Equality did not preclude gender distinctiveness; rather equality allowed their distinctiveness to be so perfectly complementary that it blended into a mysterious oneness that gloriously reflected the oneness of the Trinity. I think Theodore Roosevelt understood this symmetry when he said, "Happy homes are the responsibility of husbands and fathers—but inevitably it is wives and mothers who make it so."[2]

The man was created first, and he named the woman. The creation order and the privilege of naming the woman conferred upon the man the responsibility for headship and authority in the home (1 Timothy 2:11-13).

The woman was designed to be a helper. This did not assign an inferior position or responsibility to the woman. The Hebrew word for helper, *ezer,* is used many times throughout the Old Testament to refer to God as our *ezer.* This design enabled the woman to bring completeness to the Garden Home. (I discuss this in greater detail in my book *By Design*.)

They were one flesh. This wondrous intimacy removed Adam's aloneness and proclaimed the centrality of marriage. It is no wonder that the nineteenth-century preacher John Angell James said, "Marriage is the foundation of the domestic constitution. . . . it can never . . . be guarded with too much solicitous vigilance. . . . A married couple without mutual regard is one of the most pitiable spectacles on earth."[3]

Marriage meant leaving father and mother in order to establish this new relationship, and remember that Adam and Eve did not have a father and mother. They would *be* the father and mother. They would have offspring, and these children would leave them. This parting would not present a problem because of the oneness of their marriage. In a place of grace, relationships would be strengthened, not severed, through this process.

The man was united to his wife. This is covenant language. It is a binding commitment and pledge that reflects God's covenant commitment to His own

There was nakedness but no shame. The man and woman could face one another with no shame because they reflected only God's glory to one another. There is no shame in that.

Adam and Eve had responsibilities. The first couple could reflect God's glory to one another, and then they could turn and face creation with a unity of purpose—to obey God's cultural mandate to be fruitful and to exercise dominion over the earth.

The Garden Home was a sanctuary of grace because God was there, and He lived in unbroken fellowship with His image-bearers, the crown of His creation. Adam and Eve gazed at God's glory, and then they touched each other with the glory of that love. All of their responsibilities to each other and to creation harmonized. There was no selfishness, shame, or sorrow.

The elusiveness of this kind of sanctuary is frustrating and painful. Deep in our souls we all resonate with the reality of the words of John Angell James: "It is an unquestionable truth, that if a man be not happy at home, he cannot be happy anywhere; and the converse of the proposition is no less true, that he who *is* happy there, need be miserable nowhere."[4]

The Garden Home is out of reach for us today. We cannot fully achieve that delightful oneness because Adam sinned and all of his children are sinners. But God's Son provided a way for children of Adam to be redeemed. God's Child purchased a Heavenly Home that surpasses the Garden Home.

THE HEAVENLY HOME

Our knowledge about this home is as clouded as our knowledge of the Garden Home, but the similarities between the two are striking. Heaven is the dwelling place of God; thus it is a sanctuary of grace.

Then I saw a new heaven and a new earth, for the first heaven and the first earth had passed away, and there was no longer any sea. I saw the Holy City, the new Jerusalem, coming down out of heaven from God, prepared as a bride beautifully dressed for her husband. And I heard a loud voice from the throne saying, "Now the dwelling of God is with men, and he will live with them. They will be his people, and God himself will be with them and be their God. He will wipe every tear from their eyes. There will be no more death or mourning or crying or pain, for the old order of things has passed away."

REVELATION 21:1-4

Then the angel showed me the river of the water of life, as clear as crystal, flowing from the throne of God and of the Lamb down the middle of the great street of the city. On each side of the river stood the tree of life, bearing twelve crops of fruit, yielding its fruit every month. And the leaves of the tree are for the healing of the nations. No longer will there be any curse. The throne of God and of the Lamb will be in the city, and his servants will serve him. They will see his face, and his name will be on their foreheads. There will be no more night. They will not need the light of a lamp or the light of the sun, for the Lord God will give them light. And they will reign for ever and ever.

REVELATION 22:1-5

We know that Jesus has prepared this place for us and that He will take us there. "In my Father's house are many rooms; if it were not so, I would have told you. I am going there to prepare a place for you. And if I go and prepare a place for you, I will come back and take you to be with me that you also may be where I am" (John 14:2-3).

We know that heaven is a place where we will be welcomed because Jesus wants us to be there with Him. He even prayed for this: "Father, I want those you have given me to be with me where I am, and to see my glory, the glory you have given me because you loved me before the creation of the world" (John 17:24).

We know that we will not be on probation. We will live there forever. "Surely goodness and love will follow me all the days of my life, and I will dwell in the house of the LORD forever" (Psalm 23:6).

Zechariah records a dazzling description of our Heavenly Home. The immediate application of Zechariah's vision was for the Jews who had returned from exile in Babylon. His words would have been a great encouragement as they faced opposition and discouragement. The prophet's description offers hope for us also as we wait for its ultimate fulfillment when the Holy City, the new Jerusalem, comes down out of heaven.

> *This is what the LORD says: "I will return to Zion and dwell in Jerusalem. Then Jerusalem will be called the City of Truth, and the mountain of the LORD Almighty will be called the Holy Mountain. . . . Once again men and women of ripe old age will sit in the streets of Jerusalem, each with cane in hand because of his age. The city streets will be filled with boys and girls playing there. . . . I will save my people from the countries of the east and the west. I will bring them back to live in Jerusalem; they will be my people, and I will be faithful and righteous to them as their God."*
>
> ZECHARIAH 8:3-8

This is marvelously covenantal! There is the gathered community of God's people with God in their midst. There are men and women of ripe old age and streets filled with playful boys and girls. This is covenant life. In this City of Truth there will be no generation gaps, no guilt, no grief because God is there. We will gaze at Him and once again reflect only Him to each other. We will be His people, and He will be faithful and righteous to us, not because we deserve it but because He has bound Himself to us in covenant faithfulness.

Because of sin, we can never fully replicate our Heavenly Home on this earth, but the Christian home should be a sweet foretaste of the home that our Savior purchased and prepared for us.

We are between the Garden Home and the Heavenly Home. We cannot create heaven on earth, but when heaven is our destination, we can have homes that reflect that place. Our homes can and should be a preview of what is to come. Moses and Paul provide thrilling tutorials for this interim.

MOSES' LESSON

After God promised Moses that His presence would go with His people, Moses asked God the ultimate question. He asked to see God's glory. Moses had seen the burning bush in the desert, the plagues in Egypt, the wall of water as the Israelites walked through the sea on dry ground, the pillar of fire in the sky, and the light and sound show at Sinai. But he wanted more. "Then Moses said, 'Now show me your glory.' And the LORD said, 'I will cause all my goodness to pass in front of you . . .'" (Exodus 33:18-19).

Moses had seen the power of God, but now God showed Moses His goodness. He showed Moses the splendor of His character. God put Moses in a cleft in the rock. "And he passed in front of Moses, proclaiming, 'The LORD, the LORD, the compassionate and gracious God, slow to anger, abounding in love and faithfulness, maintaining love to thousands, and forgiving wickedness, rebellion and sin'" (Exodus 34:6-7).

God revealed Himself to Moses as the Lord, or *Yahweh*. This name proclaims the intimacy of God's relationship with His covenant people. He also revealed the goodness of His character. And look what happened. "When Moses came down from Mount Sinai with the two tablets of the Testimony in his hands, he was not aware that his face was radiant because he had spoken with the LORD" (v. 29).

This is incredible! It is incredible that Moses visibly radiated the glory of God. What is equally astonishing is that he was not even aware of it. But doesn't it have to be that way? The more I am aware of myself, the less I radiate God's character. My selfism dims the reflection of His glory. As we gaze at God's glory, we are transformed into His likeness, and we become increasingly compassionate, gracious, slow to anger, loving, faithful, and forgiving. Our homes are transformed into places of grace where the glory of His goodness radiates from the inhabitants. And make no mistake, this has nothing to do with self-effort. This is grace-zone living.

"Those who look to him are radiant; their faces are never covered with shame" (Psalm 34:5).

Jehoshaphat's prayer is so right: "We do not know what to do, but our eyes are upon you" (2 Chronicles 20:12).

No wonder the Psalmist exhorts us to "look to the LORD and his strength; seek his face always" (Psalm 105:4).

PAUL'S LESSON

In his letter to the Ephesians, Paul begins with an electrifying exposition on the person and work of the triune God. We are left breathless by his resounding doxology for the believer's blessings in Christ. Then he moves to the focus of his letter, the mystery of the church. Woven into the discussion about the family of families, the church, Paul gives instruction to individual families.

> *Be imitators of God, therefore, as dearly loved children and live a life of love, just as Christ loved us and gave himself up for us as a fragrant offering and sacrifice to God. . . .*
>
> *Submit to one another out of reverence for Christ. Wives, submit to your husbands as to the Lord. For the husband is the head of the wife as Christ is the head of the church, his body, of which he is the Savior. Now as the church submits to Christ, so also wives should submit to their husbands in everything.*
>
> *Husbands, love your wives, just as Christ loved the church and gave himself up for her to make her holy, cleansing her by the washing with water through the word, and to present her to himself as a radiant church, without stain or wrinkle or any other blemish, but holy and blameless. In this same way, husbands ought to love their wives as their own bodies. He who loves his wife loves himself. After all, no one ever hated his own body, but he feeds and cares for it, just as Christ does the church—for we are members of his body.*

"For this reason a man will leave his father and mother and be united to his wife, and the two will become one flesh." This is a profound mystery—but I am talking about Christ and the church. However, each one of you also must love his wife as he loves himself, and the wife must respect her husband.

Children, obey your parents in the Lord, for this is right. "Honor your father and mother"—which is the first commandment with a promise—"that it may go well with you and that you may enjoy long life on the earth."

Fathers, do not exasperate your children; instead, bring them up in the training and instruction of the Lord.

EPHESIANS 5:1-2, 21—6:4

In his must-read book, *Each for the Other: Marriage As It's Meant to Be,* Bryan Chapell explores the meaning and application of this passage. I hope the following quote will entice you to read the entire book.

> As the values of our secular society continue to assail our families, it becomes increasingly critical that Christian homes where God's Word is honored have an effective witness for the gospel, ensuring the spiritual well-being of the next generation. Without healthy Christian homes where the unselfish and sacrificial care of Jesus is daily demonstrated, the deep realities of the Christian faith remain mere abstractions to family members and thus fail to take root in society as a whole. . . . although the apostolic writers addressed Christians in a secular culture much like our own, their words did not call the early Christians to retreat from their society. Instead, the apostles called each Christian to retreat from self.
>
> By teaching the sacrifice of one's own priorities to the needs of a loved one, the apostles planned to beacon the truths of Christ's love in a way the world could not ignore. As we live for each other, we reenact the story of Jesus' sacrifice that lifts us from the bottomless pit of self-indulgence to a purposeful life with God.[5]

Moses and Paul push us to grace-zone living.

LIVING IN THE GRACE ZONE

Family is a profound and magnificent mystery. Nurturing a strong family is quite beyond our reach. Perhaps that is the reason we search so desperately for how-to books. The reality is, to do it God's way is an impossible task in our own strength, but that is part of the magnificence of God's way. This endeavor is designed to move us *beyond* our ability and into the realm of grace. Paul said that he wants us "to know about the grace that God has given the Macedonian churches. . . . For I testify that they gave as much as they were able, and even beyond their ability . . ." (2 Corinthians 8:1, 3).

God's grace empowers us to live beyond our ability. This kind of living pushes us beyond formulas and how-to manuals. It drives us to think about the big ideas. Where did I come from? Why am I here? Who is God, and how do I relate to Him? Living beyond our own ability also pushes us to think practically about people—specific people—and to pray for grace to show them God's goodness.

Dr. Hudson Armerding was president of Wheaton College from 1965 to 1982. This senior statesman was interviewed in a publication of Covenant Theological Seminary. In these excerpts from that interview, this wise sage who lives in the grace zone talks very practically about family. His counsel will help us to have homes that are places of grace.

The father of five children, Dr. Armerding gives his thoughts on parenting: "I learned something I should have learned a long time before—that you study your children and treat each of them uniquely depending upon the way in which God has put them together."

As a husband of fifty-four years he says:

My marriage has not been without conflict because I married a lady who is very different from myself. She has charitably reminded me that if we were the same, one of us would be unnecessary. But really, when conflicts do occur, I've tried to look beyond the conflict itself and sort out the things that matter and the things that really don't matter. There are always some things that my wife would do one way and I would do another, but it's not worth making an issue out of it. I have told many young married couples who find themselves frustrated by these differences to sort them out and deal directly and persistently only with those issues that have basic importance. There is a degree of flexibility and charity in dealing with conflicts; they don't need to become so acerbic and abrasive that it results in alienation. If you avoid that in a familial relationship, then certainly it ought to be possible elsewhere as well."

Two of the people who impacted Dr. Armerding's life are his father and a friend, Dr. Robertson McQuilkin. "My father had the habit of getting up before dawn, of reading the Word of God reflectively, and then spending extended times in prayer, and he did this each day. He claimed that he was a man of one book, the Holy Scriptures. I have been increasingly grateful for my father's devotion to the Lord and in particular to the truthfulness of the Word of God." And about Dr. McQuilkin, former president of Columbia Bible College, Dr. Armerding writes: ". . . for twenty years he has cared for his wife who has Alzheimer's. When I last saw him, he manifested again the remarkable sense of resting in the Lord and rejoicing in Him while his wife can barely respond. He delights in doing everything for her and rejoices in the fact that he has the privilege of caring for her. And so Robertson is to me a personification of living the victorious Christian life."[6]

THE LEGACY OF LOVE

Christopher and Mary Love also lived in the grace zone—far beyond their own ability. They looked past the immediate to the eternal, and they radiated God's goodness to each other and to a watching world.

Christopher Love, a brilliant young Puritan preacher, was beheaded in 1651. The story of his fearless faith and of the tender love between this man and his young pregnant wife is told by Don Kistler in *A Spectacle unto God*. Mary and Christopher Love reflected

God's glory to each other, and their marriage continues to be a beacon of what God intends for the Christian home. They were a haven of grace for each other even in the most horrific circumstances. A few days before his death, Mary Love wrote the following to her husband:

> Before I write a word further, I beseech thee think not that it is thy wife but a friend now that writes to thee. I hope thou hast freely given up thy wife and children to God, who hath said in Jeremiah 49:11, "Leave thy fatherless children, I will preserve them alive, and let thy widow trust in me." Thy Maker will be my husband, and a Father to thy children. O that the Lord would keep thee from having one troubled thought for thy relations. I desire freely to give thee up into thy Father's hands, and not only look upon it as a crown of glory for thee to die for Christ, but as an honor to me that I should have a husband to leave for Christ.
>
> I dare not speak to thee, nor have a thought within my own heart of my unspeakable loss, but wholly keep my eye fixed upon thy inexpressible and inconceivable gain. Thou leavest but a sinful, mortal wife to be everlastingly married to the Lord of glory. Thou leavest but children, brothers, and sisters to go to the Lord Jesus, thy eldest Brother. Thou leavest friends on earth to go to the enjoyment of saints and angels, and the spirits of just men made perfect in glory. Thou dost but leave earth for heaven and changest a prison for a palace. And if natural affections should begin to arise, I hope that spirit of grace that is within thee will quell them, knowing that all things here below are but dung and dross in comparison to those things that are above. I know thou keepest thine eye fixed on the hope of glory, which makes thy feet trample on the loss of earth.
>
> My dear, I know God hath not only prepared glory for thee, and thee for it, but I am persuaded that He will sweeten the way for thee to come to the enjoyment of it.

When thou art putting on thy clothes that morning, O think, "I am now putting on my wedding garments to go to be everlastingly married to my Redeemer. . . ."

My dear, by what I write unto thee, I do not hereby undertake to teach thee; for these comforts I have received from the Lord by thee. I will write no more, nor trouble thee any further, but commit thee into the arms of God with whom ere long thee and I shall be.

Farewell, my dear. I shall never see thy face more till we both behold the face of the Lord Jesus at that great day.[7]

THE ANCIENT PATH

Here is the ancient path, the good way. Meditate on it and walk in it.

Let us fix our eyes on Jesus, the author and perfecter of our faith, who for the joy set before him endured the cross, scorning its shame, and sat down at the right hand of the throne of God. Consider him who endured such opposition from sinful men, so that you will not grow weary and lose heart.

HEBREWS 12:2-3

So we fix our eyes not on what is seen, but on what is unseen. For what is seen is temporary, but what is unseen is eternal.

2 CORINTHIANS 4:18

And we, who with unveiled faces all reflect the Lord's glory, are being transformed into his likeness with ever-increasing glory, which comes from the Lord, who is the Spirit.

2 CORINTHIANS 3:18

QUESTIONS AND ANSWERS

Q. Who should initiate family devotions?

A. Ideally the husband, as head of the home, should initiate and lead in family worship. However, this should not cause dissension in the marriage. Wives sometimes become resentful because their husbands do not take the lead in this area, and that sin is at least as flagrant as the lack-of-spiritual-leadership sin. When the husband does not take this initiative, the wife should pray—a lot!—about her attitude, for wisdom to know how to deal with the situation, and for grace to be compassionate and gracious to her husband. The Lord may lead her to ask her husband if they can begin family worship, or He may lead her to quietly begin this with the children and invite her husband to participate. Sometimes husbands are hesitant or resistant because they are insecure. A wise wife will cultivate such a haven of grace that it becomes a very safe place for her husband to venture beyond his comfort zone. It may be that the process of a wife praying for grace to reflect the goodness of God to her husband is as important as beginning the family worship time.

Q. *We are first-generation Christians. Our parents do not tell our children the praiseworthy deeds of the Lord. How can we fill that void for our children?*

A. First, you have the parents, and your children have the grandparents that God ordained. Carefully guard your heart against resentment that will keep you from honoring your parents. A negative attitude about your parents will teach your children to dishonor their parents.

Then adopt a grandparent-age person or couple in your church. Invite them to your home, ask them to share stories about their childhood with your children, celebrate their birthday, and invite them to your children's birthday parties. Soon they will be spiritually grandparenting your children.

BIBLE STUDY

1. Read Exodus 33 and 34.
   • Make Moses' prayer in 33:18 your prayer.
   • What did God show Moses in 34:5-7? Make a list of these attributes of God.
   • Pray that God will give you grace to reflect these qualities to your family.
2. Read Psalm 34. Compare verse 5 with Exodus 34:29.

3. Read 1 Corinthians 13:4-7.
    - List the descriptions of love given in this passage.
    - Compare this list with your list from Exodus 34:5-7.

4. Read 2 Corinthians 3:18.

5. Read Paul's letter to the Ephesians. Pray that 5:21—6:4 will be a description of your home.

3

Purpose and Authority

TELL THE NEXT GENERATION

Paul and Georgia Settle, Dallas, Texas

Susan: *Paul and Georgia, I love the way you invest in the next genera-tion of families. Why do you spend so much time spiritually mothering and fathering young couples? Please tell us some of the things you do that will help others who want to make this same kind of investment.*

Paul and Georgia: *The Christian's greatest joy is to know God. The next is to serve Him by making Him known, especially to the next generation. In God's good providence, we, having received the truth of God from many godly men and women, have had the privilege, in our turn, of passing it on to the next generation in a great variety of ways.*

In our pastorates we have ministered to whole families—including adults, of course, but also to infants, toddlers, children, and youth. We have participated in the frolic and frenzy of vacation Bible schools, taught communicants' classes, played ball with the kids at church picnics, camped out with the guys, and taught the girls Christian decorum. We have discipled youth during Bible studies, bus trips to Bible and mission conferences, catechism classes, and many one-on-one chatting and counseling sessions. This discipling is often unplanned but occurs as we take opportunities to express our interest in or concern for individuals the Lord has brought into our lives.

Once we took a young woman into our home who had conceived out of wedlock. We shared the progress of her pregnancy and helped arrange for the adoption of her child by a grateful covenant family. This "daughter" is now the wife of a pastor and mother of their three handsome children. Other young women and men have lived with us for brief times. Some have brought great joy; others have been difficult, but the Lord has taught us much through each one.

In recent years we have been blessed by a host of young ministerial students who have regularly met in our home early on Saturday mornings for full breakfasts prepared by Georgia and for studies with Paul in the Westminster Confession of Faith. Many of these students, with their wives or girlfriends, have gathered in our home on Sunday evenings to watch and discuss videos on the roles of women in the home, church, and society.

For years Georgia has made a practice of sewing baby blankets for the new babies in our congregations. And we regularly counsel young people who are contemplating marriage or young married couples who seek guidance from the Scriptures.

Perhaps our greatest joy is felt when we learn that these young disciples are, in their turn, faithfully passing accounts of the praiseworthy deeds of the Lord on to yet another generation. To God all praise and glory!

*Forming with the church the only two institutions ever set up by God,
as to their frame work . . . it [the family] remains amidst the ruins of the fall,
the lapse of ages, and the changes of human affairs, the monument of
what has been, the standing prediction of what shall be. Tyrants that crush the
liberties of a state cannot destroy the constitution of the family; and even perse-
cutors that silence the preacher, and scatter the congregation, cannot hush
the voice of parental instruction, or extinguish parental influence.*[1]

JOHN ANGELL JAMES

In our current cultural quagmire, parents have hushed their own voices. The lack of parental influence is epidemic, systemic, and self-imposed.

The only way we can begin to recover a biblical perspective of family is to go to the very core of the problem. We must return to the ancient paths, the foundational truths. Our voices must be clear, purposeful, and substantive. We must be wise men and women who build on rock and not on sand (Matthew 7:24-27). "Each one should be careful how he builds. For no one can lay any foundation other than the one already laid, which is Jesus Christ. If any man builds on this foundation using gold, silver, costly stones, wood, hay or straw, his work will be shown for what it is, because the Day will bring it to light. It will be revealed with fire, and the fire will test the quality of each man's work" (1 Corinthians 3:10-13).

We must lay solid foundations that our children and grandchildren can build upon, and we must use imperishable materials. "For you have been born again, not of perishable seed, but of imperishable, through the living and enduring word of God. For, 'All men are like grass, and all their glory is like the flowers of the field; the grass withers and the flowers fall, but the word of the Lord stands forever'" (1 Peter 1:23-25).

Regaining our voice will mean knowing God's purpose for our family. A story told by R. C. Sproul illustrates this point. After enrolling his oldest child in public kindergarten, Dr. Sproul attended a parent-teacher meeting where the principal gave a presentation on the design of the curriculum. He told the parents that during the first fifteen minutes of the day the children played with puzzles that were scientifically designed to teach specific motor skills. He meticulously explained the purpose and function of each activity of the day and then asked if there were any questions. Everyone erupted into laughter. How could anyone possibly ask a question after his exhaustive explanation?

Dr. Sproul raised his hand. He thanked the principal for his presentation and said, "Theoretically you had an infinite number of purposes from which to select, and you had to make choices. What is your overarching purpose that determines why you make specific choices? What kind of child are you trying to produce?"

He recounts that the principal turned beet-red and then ash-white. He finally responded, "I don't know. No one has ever asked me that question."

Dr. Sproul thanked the principal for his honesty and then said, "Sir, your answer terrifies me."

It is terrifying enough that this school principal did not know the overarching purpose that determined his choices, but what is more terrifying is that most parents are just as random in their choices. We must be sure we can answer the question Dr. Sproul asked the school principal. What is the overarching purpose of our family that will determine the myriad of specific choices we will make? This will force us to ask another question: Who or what is the authority that will determine our purpose?

When the Westminster divines were crafting The Westminster Shorter Catechism, they hit these two issues head on. They began with the question: *What is the chief end of man?* They stated categorically: *Man's chief end is to glorify God, and to enjoy Him forever.*[2]

Then they addressed the authority issue by asking, *What rule hath God given to direct us how we may glorify and enjoy him?* Again there were no exceptions: *The word of God, which is contained in the Scriptures of the Old and New Testament, is the only rule to direct us how we may glorify and enjoy him.*[3]

This thinking is revolutionary to us moderns. Modernity's messages of pragmatism, relativism, and subjectivism have metastasized in our hearts. Whether or not we verbalize it, we act out our belief that the purpose for our existence is our own happiness. It will take radical repentance to cleanse our souls and our homes of this cancer.

It doesn't matter if you are a first-generation Christian and have never seen a Christian family. Noah had never seen an ark—shucks, he had never even seen rain—but he started building. And despite the ridicule from his peers, the duration of time (100 years!), and the dailyness of the task, plank by plank he built a place of safety for his family.

So must we.

Noah's boat-building project was not some wild-eyed idea about isolating his family from all the other families on the planet. It was bold obedience based on the authority of God's Word. It was substantive obedience based on God's covenant promise.

The doctrines of creation and covenant are fundamental to understanding the purpose of and authority for our lives and for our families. Cornelius Van Til wrote, "The covenant idea is based upon the concept of creation, and the concept of creation is once more based upon our idea of God. And as for our idea of God, we hold to it not as a moral or mental luxury but as the very foundation of the structure of human experience."[4]

You may be thinking, *I don't have time for the theoretical/theological. I need practical tips to help me survive a difficult marriage or three preschool children or a rebellious teen.* There is nothing more practical than knowing God. We must know Him as Creator and Redeemer in order to reflect His goodness in every relationship and situation. The practical without the theological will be form without substance, and it will be paper thin.

CREATION

The first five words of the Bible are the decisive words of the Bible. If "in the beginning God created" is true, then all the rest must be true. Since God was in the beginning, He was before the beginning. He caused the beginning. He commanded everything into existence. He made everything out of nothing. From this point on, biblical truth stands in opposition to every human-concocted conclusion about the meaning of life. Since He is the Creator, He is the Ruler, the sovereign King, the ultimate authority.

After each act of creation God said, "It is good." It was good because the Creator is good.

When everything was in place, God said, "Let us make man in our image, in our likeness" (Genesis 1:26). The sovereign King made creatures in His own image, which means that they were created to be representations and reflections of Him. The first man and woman were not God, so of course they did not reflect everything about Him any more than a mirror reflects everything about us. But they did have the capacity to reflect some things about Him. In God's words, "Let *us* make man," we catch a glimpse into the mystery of the Trinity. A triune God who has such perfect unity that He is three in one created us. The implications are pervasive. The perfection of this relationship is to be mirrored in our relationships.

Because we are in God's image, we are personal beings who have the capacity to live in union with Him and with one another. Our intimacy with Him—or lack thereof—will be reflected in our relationships with one another.

CREATION—WHAT DIFFERENCE DOES IT MAKE?

There are two approaches to faith and life—God's way and man's way. God's way is based on the truth that we were created by a personal God, we live in relationship to Him, and we are accountable to Him. His Word is absolute truth and is our rule for faith and life.

Man's way is based on the belief that there is no Creator. We live in an impersonal universe, so there is no outside authority to whom we are accountable. There is no such thing as sin, so every person determines his own standard of right and wrong. Any meaning for our existence must be derived from within ourselves, so we each become our own god.

Creation is the starting point of a biblical world- and life-view. We cannot simply go into cruise control and assume that because we are Christians, we or our children will think Christianly. Our children must be trained, and it begins with understanding the implications of creation. Dr. Van Til summarized it well: "Non-Christians believe that the universe has created God. They have a finite god. Christians believe that God has created the universe. They have a finite universe. Non-Christians therefore are not concerned with bringing the child face to face with God. They want to bring the child face to face with the universe. . . ."[5]

The creation event teaches us that God is the ultimate authority and that we were created to represent and reflect Him. This is true for individuals and families. This is not an imposition of tyranny; it is an invitation to blessedness. Abraham Kuyper takes us deep into the mystery of this blessedness:

> The blessings that come to us as a result of our being created by the Father are beyond our comprehension. Because God fashioned us fully and completely, something within us has him in it. We have something of his power, his thought, and his creative genius, characteristics that exist in no other creature made by his hands. What's more, when we're massed together, we become the whole display of his creative power, his work of art in myriad shapes and colors and sizes. We are his masterpiece. . . .
>
> To know deeply that we are children of God, the masterpieces of his handiwork—to know that we bear our Father's image and carry his likeness—brings to all who comprehend it a clear twofold understanding.

First, it brings consolation and comfort. We are his, indelibly marked with his own essence. He will love us because we are his own.

Second, it brings fear and trembling. Because we are his, our sin is not simply our own but a grievous wound on God's own essence.

To begin every morning of one's life with the knowledge that we have been created by God is the first step in realizing the importance of avoiding sin. God made us. Our unfaithfulness, in a ghastly way, wrenches his Father-heart.[6]

PUTTING PRINCIPLE INTO PRACTICE

From the time our children—and by this I mean our own children, our grandchildren, and the children in our church—can talk, they begin learning the first five questions of the *Catechism for Young Children.*

Q. 1. *Who made you?*
A. God.
Q. 2. *What else did God make?*
A. God made all things.
Q. 3. *Why did God make you and all things?*
A. For His own glory.
Q. 4. *How can you glorify God.*
A. By loving Him and doing what He commands.
Q. 5. *Why should you glorify God?*
A. Because He made me and takes care of me.[7]

Teach children and youth the biblical truth about creation. Tell them repeatedly that they are masterpieces of the Master. Their significance and purpose is derived from the magnificent reality that they are image-bearers of the Most High. Teach them to value others for this same reason. Enjoy the wonder of nature and continually tell your children that "the heavens declare the glory of God; the skies proclaim the work of his hands" (Psalm 19:1). When you visit national parks and museums, be prepared to counteract the evolution theory with biblical truth.

COVENANT

Creation shouts to us of God's glory. Covenant shouts to us of God's glorious love. The covenant motif runs throughout Scripture. The word is mentioned almost 300 times. A covenant is a binding agreement. The biblical covenants give us the framework of Scripture. Without understanding this framework, our approach to understanding and applying God's Word will be cursory and convoluted. We will be prone to the distortions of liberalism, legalism, and moralism (for a discussion of this tendency, see chapter 3 of *Heirs of the Covenant),* all of which weaken the structure of a haven of grace.

A point of clarification needs to be made. Family is a divine institution, but family is not a covenant institution. J. G. Vos explains:

> Since marriage and the family are not confined to Christian people, but are co-extensive with the human race, the family as such cannot be a covenant institution. There are families among atheists, as well as among Christians. The family is indeed a divine institution, but it is not peculiar to Christianity. . . . But in the case of Christian people, the institution of the family takes on a new significance. It is related, in their case, to the Covenant of Grace; it exists within the sphere of the Covenant of Grace. As Dr. R. J. George pointed out many years ago: "The family is a moral person. It is to be in covenant with God. It has institutions of worship peculiar to itself. It is embraced in the bosom of the church."[8]

Since the Christian family exists within the sphere of the covenant of grace, we need to have some understanding of the covenants. Even a basic grasp of the covenantal structure of Scripture will provide us with imperishable materials to build our family foundation. In Scripture there are basically three covenants—the covenant of redemption, the covenant of works, and the covenant of grace. These are not distinct from one another, but rather they are different aspects of God's plan to claim a people for Himself who will live in His presence and reflect His glory.

There are grand theological tomes written by brilliant theologians on this topic, so the idea of a theological novice compressing these covenants into a few paragraphs seems rather impertinent. I can only hope that this stimulates your theological taste buds.

THE COVENANT OF REDEMPTION

This covenant was made in eternity past between the Father, Son, and Holy Spirit. It points us to the perfect unity of the Trinity in the work of redemption. Each member of the Trinity assumed a specific redemptive task without diminishing the oneness of God's being.

The Father "chose us in him before the creation of the world to be holy and blameless in his sight. In love he predestined us to be adopted as his sons through Jesus Christ, in accordance with his pleasure and will—to the praise of his glorious grace, which he has freely given us in the One he loves" (Ephesians 1:4-6).

In Jesus "we have redemption through his blood, the forgiveness of sins, in accordance with the riches of God's grace . . ." (v. 7). Jesus is the "Lamb that was slain from the creation of the world" (Revelation 13:8).

The Holy Spirit is our "seal . . . a deposit guaranteeing our inheritance until the redemption of those who are God's possession. . ." (Ephesians 1:13, 14). And it is all for the purpose of "the praise of his glorious grace" (vv. 6, 12, 14).

We cannot begin to fathom the depth of this glorious mystery, but we can celebrate it with a life lived for God's glory. We were known and loved by God even before the beginning. Our redemption was planned, purchased, and applied by God. "The accomplishment of it is anchored to the omnipotence, unchangeability and veracity of the living God."[9]

THE COVENANT OF WORKS

This covenant was between God and Adam, but Adam did not act for himself alone. He was the representative for all mankind. In the covenant of works Adam did not do anything to earn or deserve his favored-creature status. God sovereignly determined to create a creature in His own image, thereby giving the man and woman the capacity to live in relationship with Him.

Adam and Eve were told that as long as they acknowledged God's authority by obeying His command, they would continue to live in His presence. So the covenant of works is an agreement that the relationship would be maintained as long as Adam kept the terms of the covenant—perfect obedience to God's law.

Adam and Eve chose self-rule rather than God's rule. The Fall separated Adam and Eve from God and thus from their reason for existence. They could no longer reflect God's glory. They reflected guilt and shame, and it was not a pretty picture. When God came to the garden, rather than running to greet Him, they hid. When the Lord questioned them, they began blame-shifting. "The man said, 'The woman you put here with me—she gave me some fruit from the tree, and I ate it.' Then the LORD God said to the woman, 'What is this you have done?' The woman said, 'The serpent deceived me, and I ate'" (Genesis 3:12-13).

Adam and Eve's sin would be passed to all their offspring. Every mortal born from them would carry the germ. We all are infected with that original sin. We sin because we are born with sinful natures. We are alienated from God, and so we are alienated from one another because we reflect the fallen self to each other. This was played out to its full extent in Adam and Eve's own children. Cain's jealousy erupted into full-fledged hatred, and he killed his brother Abel. When God asked, "Where is your brother Abel?" Cain replied, "I don't know. Am I my brother's keeper?" (Genesis 4:9).

Because of sin, we want to be our own authority. We live for self-interest. We do not assume responsibility for one another. It's the sinful way. It's the way of worldlings.

We cannot avoid the reality of sin. We can deny it. We can rationalize it. We can excuse it. But the self-evident reality is, we and our progeny are sinners. Homes without the redemptive mercy of Jesus become sepulchers of shame, sorrow, blame-shifting, and hostility, rather than sanctuaries of grace.

And the Fall rendered us powerless to do anything about our predicament. "For the wages of sin is death . . ." (Romans 6:23).

You don't get more powerless than that.

THE COVENANT OF GRACE

When Adam and Eve chose self-governance, it should have been the end of human history, but instead it became the revelation of redemptive history. Adam and Eve lost the privilege and the ability to live in God's presence. They could not undo what they had done. They did not deserve to live in God's presence, and they could not earn their way back into His presence.

"Then the man and his wife heard the sound of the LORD God as he was walking in the garden in the cool of the day. . . . But the LORD God called to the man, 'Where are you?'" (Genesis 3:8-9). God *came*. He did not turn away from them and leave them in the darkness of their despair. He *called*, not to destroy them, but to give a promise. He said that the offspring of the woman would crush Satan's head, and Satan would strike this offspring's heel.

There was hope! God was not going to end history. He even promised that they would have children, and somewhere, sometime, one of their descendants would undo what they had done.

Then God gave them an object lesson. "The LORD God made garments of skin for Adam and his wife and clothed them" (v. 21). God *clothed* them. He covered their guilt and shame. In essence God said, "I will still be your God, I will take you as my very own, and I will make a way for your sin to be covered so that you can once again live in My presence." This is the covenant of grace.

Theologians have written splendid explanations of this covenant. Let's look at some of their grand statements. The Westminster divines wrote: "The distance between God and the creature is so great, that although reasonable creatures do owe obedience unto Him as their Creator, yet they could never have any fruition of Him as their blessedness and reward, but by some voluntary condescension on God's part, which He hath been pleased to express by way of covenant."[10]

Louis Berkhof wrote: "We generally speak of the covenant of grace as being that gracious compact or agreement between the offended God and the offending sinner, in which God promises salvation through faith in Christ and the sinner accepts this believingly."[11]

John Gerstner wrote: "The covenant of grace is the means by which the covenant of redemption is actually carried out. In the latter, salvation is agreed upon; in the former the way of salvation is settled. . . . The covenant of grace is nothing other than the way by which God decrees to carry out what he has committed himself to do. He is already bound by his decree; this covenant can bind him no tighter. It binds him more specifically. That is, it binds him with respect to a particular plan, which he has imposed upon himself. . . . The covenant of redemption was the covenant wherein it was agreed that the Son would become the mediator of the elect; and the covenant of grace was the way in which he would carry out his mediation for the elect."[12]

The covenant of grace is the sovereignly initiated arrangement whereby sinners are restored to a relationship with the God of heaven and earth. In this covenant Christ is our representative. "For there is one God and one mediator between God and men, the man Christ Jesus" (1 Timothy 2:5).

The condition to live in God's presence is the same for us as it was for Adam and Eve in the garden—perfect obedience. The terms of the covenant must be met. Our first representative was a covenant breaker, but Jesus kept the covenant terms for His people. This is grace—God's kindness, love, and mercy to undeserving sinners.

"For this reason Christ is the mediator of a new covenant, that those who are called may receive the promised eternal inheritance—now that He has died as a ransom to set them free from the sins committed under the first covenant" (Hebrews 9:15).

COVENANT—WHAT DIFFERENCE DOES IT MAKE?

Answering this question pitches us back to the purpose for our existence and the authority for our faith and life. It is the character of God that determined the purpose of our creation. He is good, so the purpose for which He created us is good. Creating us for His own glory was not inconsistent with seeking our good, because sharing His glory is as good as it gets. There is no better purpose for which God could have created us. This is magnificently probed in Dr. John Gerstner's book on Jonathan Edwards. Read, reread, and revel in this quote from Jonathan Edwards:

> In the creature's knowing, esteeming, loving, rejoicing in, and praising God, the glory of God is both exhibited and acknowledged; his fullness is received and returned. . . . The refulgence shines upon and into the creature, and is reflected back to the luminary. The beams of glory come from God, and are something of God, and are refunded back again to their original. So the whole is *of* God, and *in* God, and *to* God; and God is the beginning, middle, and end in this affair. . . . the first step in the working out of human salvation was the covenant of redemption.[13]

Sin separated us from the "beams of glory," rendering us powerless to fulfill the very purpose for our existence. The covenant *provides the way* for us to again live in the presence of glory and thus to fulfill our reason for being—reflecting that glory. "Jesus answered, 'I am the way and the truth and the life. No one comes to the Father except through me'" (John 14:6).

The covenant *provides the power* to fulfill our purpose. "For I am not ashamed of the gospel of Christ, for it is the power of God to salvation for everyone who believes, for the Jew first and also for the Greek" (Romans 1:16-17 NKJV).

The covenant *provides the motivation.* "For Christ's love compels us . . ." (2 Corinthians 5:14).

As we begin to understand the covenantal framework of

Scripture, we begin to comprehend the purpose, harmony, and connections of Scripture. We begin to apprehend that it is all about Jesus. We begin to understand that the ultimate question of life is how we relate to Him, for it is "in him [that] we live and move and have our being" (Acts 17:28). "For from him and through him and to him are all things. To him be the glory forever! Amen" (Romans 11:36).

The authority issue is also settled. "The Son is the radiance of God's glory and the exact representation of his being, sustaining all things by his powerful word. After he had provided purification for sins, he sat down at the right hand of the Majesty in heaven" (Hebrews 1:3). The one who sits at the right hand of the Majesty in heaven said, "All authority in heaven and on earth has been given to me" (Matthew 28:18).

The written Word possesses the authority of the Living Word because it is His Word. "For the word of God is living and active. Sharper than any double-edged sword, it penetrates even to dividing soul and spirit, joints and marrow; it judges the thoughts and attitudes of the heart" (Hebrews 4:12).

PUTTING PRINCIPLE INTO PRACTICE

Speak of the covenant to your children. Tell them of God's grace in your life. Tell them that we do not belong to this world, but we are God's covenant people. Let them hear you praying that they will be covenant-keepers and that they will live for God's glory. Teach them from a covenant perspective. (Chapter 3 of *Heirs of the Covenant* discusses this.)

An understanding of the covenant unifies, integrates, and harmonizes all of life. It really does matter. Christopher Love knew this.

THE LEGACY OF LOVE

Christopher and Mary Love had settled the purpose/authority issue. Their purpose was God's glory—no matter what. They lived under the authority of His Word—no matter what. In his final letter to his pregnant wife, Mary, Christopher Love wrote:

> *From the Tower of London*
> *August 22, 1651*
> *The Day of My Glorification*
>
> *My most gracious beloved,*
> *I am now going from a prison to a palace. I have finished my work; I am now to receive my wages. I am now going to heaven where are two of my children, and leaving thee on the earth where are three of my babes. Those two above need not my care, but the three below need thine. It comforts me to think two of my children are in the bosom of Abraham, and three of them will be in the arms and care of so tender and godly a mother.*
> *I know thou art a woman of a sorrowful spirit, yet be comforted; though thy sorrow be great for thy husband's going out of the world, yet thy pains shall be the less in bringing thy child into the world. Thou shalt be a joyful mother, though thou beest a sad widow. God hath many mercies in store for thee; the prayers of a dying husband for thee will not be lost. To my shame I speak it: I never prayed so much for thee at liberty as I have done in prison. I cannot write more, but I have a few practical counsels to leave with thee:*
> *1. Keep under a sound, orthodox and soul-searching ministry. Oh, there are deceivers gone out into the world, but Christ's sheep know His voice, and a stranger will they not follow. Attend on that ministry that teaches the way of God in truth, and follow Solomon's advice, Proverbs 19:27: "Cease to hear instruction that causes to err from the ways of knowledge."*
> *2. Bring up thy children in the knowledge and admonition of the Lord. . . .*
> *3. Pray in thy family daily, that thy dwelling may be in the number of the families that call upon God.*
> *4. Labor for a meek and quiet spirit, which is in the sight of God of great price, 1 Peter 3:4.*
> *5. Pour not on the comforts thou wantest, but on the mercies thou hast.*
> *6. Look rather at God's end in afflicting than at the measure and degree of thy affliction.*

7. Labor to clear up thy evidences for heaven when God takes from thee the comforts of earth, that as thy sufferings do abound, so thy consolations in Christ may abound much more, 2 Corinthians 1:5.

8. Though it is good to maintain a holy jealousy of the deceitfulness of thy heart, yet it is evil for thee to cherish fears and doubts about the truth of thy graces. If ever I had confidence touching the grace of another, I have confidence of grace in thee. . . . I could venture my soul in thy soul's stead, such a confidence I have of thee.

9. When thou findest thy heart secure, presumptuous and proud, then pour upon corruption more than upon grace; but when thou findest thy heart doubting and unbelieving, then look on thy grace, not on thy infirmities.

10. Study the covenant of grace and the merits of Christ, and then be troubled if thou canst. Thou art interested in such a covenant that accepts purposes for performances, desires for deeds, sincerity for perfection, the righteousness of another, that of Jesus Christ, as if it were thine own. Oh my love! Rest, rest, then, in the love of God, in the bosom of Christ. . . .[14]

THE ANCIENT PATH

Here is the ancient path, the good way. Meditate on it and walk in it.

For you are a people holy to the LORD your God. The LORD your God has chosen you out of all the peoples on the face of the earth to be his people, his treasured possession. The LORD did not set his affection on you and choose you because you were more numerous than other peoples, for you were the fewest of all peoples. But it was because the LORD loved you and kept the oath he swore to your forefathers that he brought you out with a mighty hand and redeemed you from the land of slavery, from the power of Pharaoh king of Egypt. Know therefore that the LORD your God is God; he is the faithful God, keeping his covenant of love to a thousand generations of those who love him and keep his commands.

DEUTERONOMY 7:6-9

QUESTIONS AND ANSWERS

Q. How do we apply the purpose/authority issues to our family life?

A. Husbands and wives must ask themselves hard questions, and they must give honest answers. Begin by asking the question R. C. Sproul asked the school principal. What is your overarching purpose that determines why you make specific choices for your family? What kind of marriage do you want? What kind of child are you trying to produce?

It is easy to rattle off the right answer, but pray David's prayer together: "Search me, O God, and know my heart; test me and know my anxious thoughts. See if there is any offensive way in me, and lead me in the way everlasting" (Psalm 139:23-24). Then discuss questions such as:

• Is our oneness purely sentimental and emotional, or is it because of our single purpose to glorify God and to live under the authority of His Word?

• Is the purpose of our marriage so firmly rooted in our desire to glorify God that even when we hit rough spots, even when we really don't like each other, we are committed to the marriage for the sake of God's glory?

• Will we be satisfied with children who avoid drugs, graduate from college, marry well, and make us proud? Or is the passion of our hearts to see our children love and serve Jesus with all their hearts?

• Are we willing to bring every decision under the authority of God's Word?

Without the purpose/authority anchor, our families will lack stability and maturity. Sometimes the rush of life and responsibilities makes us feel as if we are just along for the ride—doing what has to be done with no time to think about why we are doing it. That is normal. But if you have had the above conversation and made the purpose/authority decision, you can look at each other as you rock a sick child, or as you face the reality of a financial crisis, or when one has deeply wounded the other, and say, "We will survive this by God's grace and for His glory."

Q. If we make this commitment to live for God's glory and under the authority of His Word, will that be an end to our conflicts?

A. No! We are sinners, and we live with sinners. But what this commitment does mean is that we have a basis to look at each situation, decision, and conflict and say, "How can we glorify God through this?" We can ask God for grace to reflect His mercy to each other even when we disagree. We can ask Him for wisdom to see His way and not our own way.

Q. What application does this have to the single person?

A. These biblical truths are to be brought to bear upon our lives regardless of life season or circumstance.

BIBLE STUDY

1. Read the following verses and find the recurring promise:
   Genesis 17:7
   Exodus 6:7
   Leviticus 11:45
   Leviticus 26:12
   Deuteronomy 7:6
   Deuteronomy 29:12-13
   Jeremiah 24:7
   Jeremiah 31:33
   Zechariah 8:8
   2 Corinthians 6:16
   Titus 2:14
   Hebrews 8:10
   Revelation 21:3

2. Read Ephesians 1 and 2 every day for a week.
   • List what you learn about the character of God.
   • List what He has done for you.
   • What is the recurring phrase in verses 6, 12, and 14?
   • After a week, write a prayer of thanksgiving to Him.

4

Marriage

TELL THE NEXT GENERATION

Mark and Barbara Thompson, Zachary, Louisiana

Susan: *Mark and Barbara, your marriage is a beautiful example of the oneness God intends husbands and wives to enjoy. What are some of the things you have learned that you would like to tell the next generation?*

Mark and Barbara: *We married for all the right reasons. We had known each other for most of our lives. We even sang together in junior choir. We were church kids and later young adults who had admittedly made detours, some of which were public. The adage applied was, "they have sown their wild oats but will now settle down and return to the church."*

But in our case that cultural expectation did not prove true. We reaped what we had sown. We were captivated by the "isms" of the sixties and not by the biblical truths of the covenant of redemption or the covenant of marriage. Both of us continued acting with evil intent toward God, one another, and our marriage. Humanly speaking, we did everything within our power to destroy our marriage.

When Jesus arrested us, He began not only the individual work of sanctification but also the redemption of our marriage. He continues to use even what we intended for evil for our good and His glory. Our marriage is a monument to His mercy.

We want the next generation to know that marriage is a covenantal relationship established by God and that the vows made are to God. We will give account of our marriage vow before the Lord. Our testimony of God's grace is centered on living out marriage vows today, not tomorrow or when a certain event occurs or when behaviors are modified. Marriage is, by command of the Creator, spiritual. Christian marriage is not just "making Christ the center" so that humans may be happy. Marriage has the kingdom purpose of glorifying God and making His glory known to the next generation.

We desire to be intentional in teaching the next generations that of all human relationships, marriage is the primary one that God designated and ordained to preach the Gospel. The next generations will absorb a perspective of how Christ loves the church by the testimony of the sacrificial love of Christian husbands for their wives. The next generations will absorb a perspective of the church's submission to Christ by the testimony of the submissive respect of Christian wives for their husbands. Parenting techniques, evangelistic tools, discipleship and youth ministry models can only complement, not substitute for, the power of the Gospel lived out through the mystery and wonder of godly marriages. Marriage is God's primary design for evangelizing the next generations and glorifying Himself. Marriages count for eternity in God's kingdom purposes!

We should all enter the married state remembering that
we are about to be united to a fallen creature. . . it is not two angels
that have met together, but two sinful children of Adam.[1]

JOHN ANGELL JAMES

*N*ow the rubber meets the road. If home is going to be a place of grace, all roads lead to the marriage.

A word to those who are not married. This chapter is important for you for two reasons. First, it may be God's plan for you to be married at some point in your life. Second, you are to pray for and encourage your friends who are married to be obedient in their marriages. One of my all-time favorite books is *Aunt Jane's Hero,* a novel by Elizabeth Prentiss that presents a biblical perspective of the Christian home. Laced through this lovely romance is the positive influence of an elderly woman known affectionately as Aunt Jane. Oh for more Aunt Janes who will encourage and equip God's people for the ministry of marriage.

For the divorced, this chapter is not intended to slay you with guilt. Hopefully it will teach you about grace.

So what do I say in one chapter that can possibly help us navigate the maze called marriage? I think it would be easier to write ten volumes on the topic than to distill it down to one issue. Perhaps because the one issue that is the heart of the matter exposes the heart of us all.

ONENESS

In Scripture the synonym for marriage is oneness. In this synthesis neither partner will become less or weaker. Neither will lose anything of value. But this fusion will not be easy. There will probably be many explosions along the way.

The enemy of oneness is pride. Pride divides. Always. Pride is a trivial pursuit of self-interest. It was pride that slithered into Eve's heart and caused her to declare her independence. Autonomy never produces oneness. So how can two fallen creatures, two children of Adam, ever achieve the bliss of oneness?

We are usually as naïve and sentimental about marriage as the people who listened to Joshua's farewell address. Modern speechwriters would agree that he struck a home run in that speech. His famous sound bite is framed and hanging in many Christian homes:

> *But as for me and my household, we will serve the LORD.*
>   JOSHUA 24:15

I'm confident that Joshua never intended for anyone to take his statement out of context and sentimentalize it. This was a time of covenant renewal. Joshua threw down the gauntlet when he told the people they could serve the God of covenant faithfulness, or they could serve foreign gods, but there could be no mixing and mingling. It was one or the other. And the decision was not a private matter. It was a family matter, and it was a community matter. The people responded with zeal: "We too will serve the LORD, because he is our God" (v. 18).

Then Joshua dropped a bombshell: "You are not able to serve the LORD. He is a holy God; he is a jealous God" (v. 19). Words come easy. Joshua was pressing the people to understand that we cannot satisfy the demands of God's holiness. Marriage is a union of two fallen creatures who are not capable of serving the Lord. In ourselves we cannot achieve a oneness that will illustrate the love Jesus has for His bride, the church. We cannot overcome the pride of life.

Dr. Edmund Clowney, professor of practical theology (emeritus) at Westminster Theological Seminary, writes as only he can:

> Our only claim to the Father's mercy is the sacrifice of the Savior. Jesus became last that the last of lost sinners might be first in glory with Him. . . . Pride is not biodegradable. It

will not self-destruct. Only the Cross is the death of our pride. It must be broken there, to dissolve in tears of penitence. Only then can we take the towel, gird ourselves with humility, and begin to serve one another in the love of Christ.[2]

Pride divides, but the cross unites.

For our household to be a haven of grace where King Jesus is honored and served, there must be oneness in the marriage. Division in the marriage is evidence of mixing and mingling with foreign gods. Whether it is the god of addiction, lust, greed, selfishness, or expectations, ultimately it is the pride of life, and it erodes oneness.

Many people approach marriage the way I approach tennis. I would love to play tennis. There is a grace and beauty about the game that I find appealing. Also I like the cute clothes players wear, though I admit I would not be a pretty sight in those little skirts. Now the truth is, I know nothing about the game. I have never taken the time to learn which lines the ball is supposed to stay within or what you have to do to score a point—by this time it is obvious to tennis buffs that I do not even know the terminology. It is also obvious that I am attracted to the end product of being an agile, well-toned athlete, but I have not invested the hard work of studying the history and rules of the game or exercising the discipline of training and practicing. At least the system prohibits me from walking out on the court at Wimbledon. Not so with marriage. Unfortunately many are in the game before they realize they know nothing about the history, rules, or discipline. Is it any wonder they don't last for one inning—or whatever you call it.

THE THREE R'S

Marriage is a covenant, and the Christian marriage is to exist within the *realm*, according to the *rubric,* and under the *rules* of the covenant.

The prophet Malachi spoke to a people who doubted God's love and consequently had become slack in their obedience. When their relationship to God became casual, their relationships with one another became corrupt. Malachi's mission was to remind these people of God's covenant love and their covenant obligations. The book begins: "An oracle: The word of the LORD to Israel through Malachi. 'I have loved you,' says the LORD. 'But you ask, "How have you loved us?"'" (Malachi 1:1-2).

God answers by reminding Israel of the covenant. Then He points to the root of the problem—unfaithful priests and a lack of knowledge of God's Word: "'For the lips of a priest ought to preserve knowledge, and from his mouth men should seek instruction—because he is the messenger of the LORD Almighty. But you have turned from the way and by your teaching have caused many to stumble; you have violated the covenant with Levi,' says the LORD Almighty" (Malachi 2:7-8).

This corruption spread among the people. When they broke covenant with God, their human relationships suffered.

> *Have we not all one Father? Did not one God create us? Why do we profane the covenant of our fathers by breaking faith with one another? Judah has broken faith. A detestable thing has been committed in Israel and in Jerusalem: Judah has desecrated the sanctuary the LORD loves, by marrying the daughter of a foreign god.*
>
> *As for the man who does this, whoever he may be, may the LORD cut him off from the tents of Jacob—even though he brings offerings to the LORD Almighty.*
>
> *Another thing you do: You flood the LORD's altar with tears. You weep and wail because he no longer pays attention to your offerings or accepts them with pleasure from your hands. You ask, "Why?" It is because the LORD is acting as the witness between you and the wife of your youth, because you have broken faith with her, though she is your partner, the wife of your marriage covenant.*
>
> *Has not the LORD made them one? In flesh and spirit they are his. And why one? Because he was seeking godly offspring. So guard yourself in your spirit, and do not break faith with the wife of your youth.*

"I hate divorce," says the LORD God of Israel, "and I hate a man's covering himself with violence as well as with his garment," says the LORD Almighty. "So guard yourself in your spirit, and do not break faith."

MALACHI 2:10-16

The men broke faith with God by marrying women who worshiped foreign gods. They broke the marriage covenant, thus jeopardizing their offspring by robbing them of the example of covenant oneness. As Joshua had warned, they were "not able to serve the LORD. He is a holy God; he is a jealous God" (Joshua 24:19).

But Malachi quickly reminded the people of the provision of the covenant: "the messenger of the covenant" (3:1) who would purify the people. God called them to repentance: "'Return to me, and I will return to you,' says the LORD Almighty" (Malachi 3:7). He reaffirmed the covenant promise in all its fullness: "'They will be mine,' says the LORD Almighty, 'in the day when I make up my treasured possession'" (3:17). The extraordinary closing words of the Old Testament are the segue to the New Testament.

"Surely the day is coming; it will burn like a furnace. All the arrogant and every evildoer will be stubble, and that day that is coming will set them on fire," says the LORD Almighty. "Not a root or a branch will be left to them. But for you who revere my name, the sun of righteousness will rise with healing in its wings. And you will go out and leap like calves released from the stall. Then you will trample down the wicked; they will be ashes under the soles of your feet on the day when I do these things," says the LORD Almighty.

"Remember the law of my servant Moses, the decrees and laws I gave him at Horeb for all Israel. See, I will send you the prophet Elijah before that great and dreadful day of the LORD comes. He will turn the hearts of the fathers to their children, and the hearts of the children to their fathers; or else I will come and strike the land with a curse."

MALACHI 4

Joshua was right. We are not *able* to serve the Lord, but *God* will turn the hearts of the fathers to their children and the hearts of the children to their fathers. The gospel of grace will accomplish for us and in us what we cannot do in our own strength, and a result will be family solidarity.

Malachi warned that the integrity of the covenant community is threatened when marriage covenants are broken. The covenant community has a stake in the marriage, and the marriage needs the instruction and support of the community. When God's people do not follow covenant principles and rules, everyone suffers. The land is struck with a curse. No wonder Paul challenged the church to supply godly older women who would "train the younger women to love their husbands and children . . . so that no one will malign the word of God" (Titus 2:4-5). Older women teaching younger women how to love their husbands and children is a covenant matter.

The Christian marriage is to exist within the *realm* of the covenant community.

The *rubric* is the principle of grace: "The grace of our Lord was poured out on me abundantly, along with the faith and love that are in Christ Jesus. Here is a trustworthy saying that deserves full acceptance: Christ Jesus came into the world to save sinners—of whom I am the worst" (1 Timothy 1:14-15).

The *rule* is God's royal law of love: "If you really keep the royal law found in Scripture, 'Love your neighbor as yourself,' you are doing right" (James 2:8). Our closest neighbor is our spouse.

PORTRAIT OF A COVENANT MARRIAGE

The example of Ruth and Boaz is much more than a tender love story. It is a celebration of our redemption. It is an illustration of the three R's of covenant marriage.

When the Israelites conquered the promised land under Joshua's leadership, every family was given a parcel of land. The land was part of the promise, and the hope of the Israelites was that their offspring would live on the land until Messiah came. The land was their guarantee of sharing in the glory of Messiah.

The book of Ruth begins by reporting a famine in Israel. A man named Elimelech lacked the faith to remain steadfast through this tribulation. He temporarily relinquished his inheritance and sought relief in Moab. His wife, Naomi, and their two sons accompanied him. During their sojourn in Moab, the sons married Moabite women. Elimelech and both sons died. Then Naomi decided to return to Israel.

I find this remarkable. It makes me wonder if she ever wanted to leave Israel. Did she follow her husband in obedience to her covenant marriage vows even when her heart was breaking and her hope dissolving because she was being wrenched from their token of the covenant? Scripture does not tell us this, but it does tell us that when she decided to return to Israel, her daughter-in-law Ruth went with her. This, too, is remarkable. Mother-in-law jokes are legion, but the reality is that often relationships between women and their mothers-in-law are nothing to joke about. Many women have great difficulty releasing their son to another woman. They shrewdly and skillfully undermine the young wife while the young husband is oblivious to the war being waged between the two women.

Apparently Naomi did not play this kind of war game. I envision her as a Titus 2 woman who not only taught her spiritual daughters how to love their husbands, but who taught her sons how to love their wives. She also must have told such stories of her homeland that one of the young women was willing to leave her own land to follow her. When Naomi encouraged her daughters-in-law to remain in Moab among their own people and reminded them that she could not possibly produce sons for them to marry, Orpah returned.

However Ruth clung, not just to Naomi, but to Naomi's God: "Don't urge me to leave you or to turn back from you. Where you go I will go, and where you stay I will stay. Your people will be my people and your God my God. Where you die I will die, and there I will be buried. May the LORD deal with me, be it ever so severely, if anything but death separates you and me" (Ruth 1:16-17).

It was Naomi's God, the Lord, the God of covenant faithfulness, that Ruth embraced. This is the heart of the matter. Somehow through the intricacies of the mother-in-law relationship and the trials of widowhood, Naomi reflected God's goodness to Ruth, and there was no turning back for this young woman. Going with Naomi to the realm of the covenant meant identifying herself with the people of the covenant.

When the two widows arrived in Bethlehem, Ruth went to ask permission to pick up grain left behind by reapers. God sovereignly led Ruth to the field of a man who honored the covenant requirement to care for the aliens, fatherless, and widows.

The law stipulated: "When you are harvesting in your field and you overlook a sheaf, do not go back to get it. Leave it for the alien, the fatherless and the widow, so that the LORD your God may bless you in all the work of your hands. . . . Remember that you were slaves in Egypt. That is why I command you to do this" (Deuteronomy 24:19, 22).

The owner of the field inquired about Ruth's identity. He was touched by Ruth's choice for the covenant, and he offered her provision and protection in his fields. In the ensuing conversation, Ruth and Boaz reflect the grace of the covenant to one another.

So Boaz said to Ruth, "My daughter, listen to me. Don't go and glean in another field and don't go away from here. Stay here with my servant girls. Watch the field where the men are harvesting, and follow along after the girls. I have told the men not to touch you. And whenever you are thirsty, go and get a drink from the water jars the men have filled."

At this, she bowed down with her face to the ground. She exclaimed, "Why have I found such favor in your eyes that you notice me—a foreigner?"

Boaz replied, "I've been told all about what you have done for your mother-in-law since the death of your husband—how you left your father and mother and your homeland and came to live with a people you did not know before. May the LORD repay you for what you have done. May you be richly rewarded by the

> LORD, *the God of Israel, under whose wings you have come to*
> *take refuge."*
>   *"May I continue to find favor in your eyes, my Lord," she said.*
> *"You have given me comfort and have spoken kindly to your ser-*
> *vant—though I do not have the standing of one of your servant girls."*
>
> RUTH 2:8-13

That night Naomi was delighted with Ruth's bushel of barley,
but she was ecstatic when she learned the name of the landowner.
"'The LORD bless him!' Naomi said to her daughter-in-law. 'He has
not stopped showing his kindness to the living and the dead.' She
added, 'That man is our close relative; he is one of our kinsman-
redeemers'" (v. 20).

We must look to the corporate nature of the covenant to understand Naomi's joy. God's people had responsibilities toward one
another. They were their brother's keepers, and there were provisions
for regaining lost land and caring for widows.

> *"Throughout the country that you hold as a possession, you must*
> *provide for the redemption of the land. If one of your countrymen*
> *becomes poor and sells some of his property, his nearest relative is*
> *to come and redeem what his countryman has sold."*
>
> LEVITICUS 25:24-25

> *"If brothers are living together and one of them dies without a son,*
> *his widow must not marry outside the family. Her husband's*
> *brother shall take her and marry her and fulfill the duty of a*
> *brother-in-law to her. The first son she bears shall carry on the*
> *name of the dead brother so that his name will not be blotted out*
> *from Israel."*
>
> DEUTERONOMY 25:5-6

Naomi trained Ruth in the ways of the covenant. Ruth followed
Naomi's instructions, went to the threshing floor at night after Boaz
was asleep, and lay at his feet.

> *In the middle of the night something startled the man, and he*
> *turned and discovered a woman lying at his feet. "Who are you?"*
> *he asked.*
> *"I am your servant Ruth," she said. "Spread the corner of your*
> *garment over me, since you are a kinsman-redeemer."*
> *"The LORD bless you, my daughter," he replied. "This*
> *kindness is greater than that which you showed earlier: You*
> *have not run after the younger men, whether rich or poor. And*
> *now, my daughter, don't be afraid. I will do for you all you ask.*
> *All my fellow townsmen know that you are a woman of noble*
> *character."*

RUTH 3:8-11

Boaz redeemed the land and married Ruth, and it was a community affair.

> *Then Boaz announced to the elders and all the people, "Today you*
> *are witnesses that I have bought from Naomi all the property of*
> *Elimelech, Kilion and Mahlon. I have also acquired Ruth the*
> *Moabitess, Mahlon's widow, as my wife, in order to maintain the*
> *name of the dead with his property, so that his name will not dis-*
> *appear from among his family or from the town records. Today you*
> *are witnesses!"*
> *Then the elders and all those at the gate said, "We are witnesses.*
> *May the LORD make the woman who is coming into your home*
> *like Rachel and Leah, who together built up the house of Israel.*
> *May you have standing in Ephrathah and be famous in*
> *Bethlehem."*

RUTH 4:9-11

She was and he did. Ruth and Boaz were the great-grandparents
of David and are listed in the genealogy of Jesus (Matthew 1:3).

This story has all the right stuff:

• People who are "profoundly affected by their inescapable connection to place, persons, and principles—the incremental parts of a
covenant community."

•An older woman who understood her covenant calling to spiritually mother younger women.

•A younger woman with a teachable spirit who clung to the God of covenant faithfulness though doing so appeared to eliminate any hope of marriage and a family.

•A compassionate man who protected and provided for a stranger and alien.

•A godly man who was willing to assume his covenant responsibilities.

•A couple who shared a common purpose—their love for God's covenant and their desire to obey Him.

•A community who rejoiced with those who rejoiced and celebrated this covenant marriage.

•A covenant marriage that brought blessing to the community, for it was in Bethlehem that their descendant, *our* Kinsman-Redeemer, was born.

But don't miss the essential element of this story. Ruth and Boaz embraced the covenant because they were embraced by the God of the covenant.

EMBRACED BY GRACE

Ruth's request that Boaz "spread the corner of your garment over me" is a request for marriage. She was asking him to be the redeemer of her forfeited inheritance.

Ezekiel tells a poignant allegory that is a description of God's lavish generosity to Israel, and ultimately of His sovereign grace and mercy in spreading His garment over us. Read this story and realize that we are that unwanted infant who was abandoned and left to die.

> *The word of the LORD came to me: "Son of man, confront Jerusalem with her detestable practices and say, 'This is what the Sovereign LORD says to Jerusalem: Your ancestry and birth were in the land of the Canaanites; your father was an Amorite and your mother a Hittite.*

"'On the day you were born your cord was not cut, nor were you washed with water to make you clean, nor were you rubbed with salt or wrapped in cloths. No one looked on you with pity or had compassion enough to do any of these things for you. Rather, you were thrown out into the open field, for on the day you were born you were despised.

"'Then I passed by and saw you kicking about in your blood, and as you lay there in your blood I said to you, "Live!" I made you grow like a plant of the field. You grew up and developed and became the most beautiful of jewels. Your breasts were formed and your hair grew, you who were naked and bare.

"'Later I passed by, and when I looked at you and saw that you were old enough for love, I spread the corner of my garment over you and covered your nakedness. I gave you my solemn oath and entered into a covenant with you, declares the Sovereign LORD, and you became mine.

"'I bathed you with water and washed the blood from you and put ointments on you. I clothed you with an embroidered dress and put leather sandals on you. I dressed you in fine linen and covered you with costly garments. I adorned you with jewelry: I put bracelets on your arms and a necklace around your neck, and I put a ring on your nose, earrings on your ears and a beautiful crown on your head. So you were adorned with gold and silver; your clothes were of fine linen and costly fabric and embroidered cloth. Your food was fine flour, honey and olive oil. You became very beautiful and rose to be a queen.

"And your fame spread among the nations on account of your beauty, because the splendor I had given you made your beauty perfect,' declares the Sovereign LORD."

EZEKIEL 16:1-14

Jesus, our Kinsman-Redeemer, spreads the corner of His garment of righteousness over us. Now we can boldly say, "But as for me and my household, we will serve the LORD" (Joshua 24:15).

And when Joshua challenges us, "You are not able to serve the LORD. He is a holy God; he is a jealous God" (v. 19), we can respond,

"I delight greatly in the LORD; my soul rejoices in my God. For he has clothed me with garments of salvation and arrayed me in a robe of righteousness, as a bridegroom adorns his head like a priest, and as a bride adorns herself with her jewels" (Isaiah 61:10).

I know I have not dealt with all the issues we generally think about when we consider marriage. But it seems to me that if we begin to understand that despite our wretched condition we have been embraced by grace, we will begin to embrace our spouse in grace. Humility will replace pride, and we will begin to serve rather than expecting to be served. Oneness will flourish. Our marriages will begin to reflect the magnificence of grace rather than the mediocrity of selfishness.

SOARING THE HEIGHTS

How do we lift our marriages out of the muck of mediocrity? Strange, but it begins with brokenness. It's the pride thing again.

When Boaz and Ruth's great-grandson King David walked on his roof, he was not just on top of his palace—he was on top of the world. Apparently the thin air of power and prestige lulled him into believing he was above the law. Pride blinded David. His adultery, murder, and cover-up are well known.

Nathan the prophet confronted David with his sin, David's spiritual eyes were opened, he saw things as they really were, and he said, "I have sinned against the LORD" (2 Samuel 12:13). His prayer of repentance in Psalm 51 is a portion of Scripture we should all live in frequently, for it is the prayer we all need to pray continually.

God forgave David, but there were consequences to his sin: "Nathan replied, 'The LORD has taken away your sin. You are not going to die. But because by doing this you have made the enemies of the LORD show utter contempt, the son born to you will die.' After Nathan had gone home, the LORD struck the child that Uriah's wife had borne to David, and he became ill. David pleaded with God for the child. He fasted and went into his house and spent the nights lying on the ground" (2 Samuel 12:13-16).

David's grief was so intense over the illness of his son that when the child died, his servants were afraid to tell him. But David knew, and he surprised everyone when he got up from the ground, washed, changed his clothes, and went to the house of the Lord and worshiped. This account is so loaded that we often miss what happened next: "Then David comforted his wife Bathsheba . . ." (v. 24). This is the fruit of thorough repentance—wondrous worship and gentle grace.

David did not need to take a sensitivity-training course. He repented, worshiped, and then ministered to his wife. A telling evidence of true repentance is a keen awareness of others' needs and a sanctified understanding of how to touch those needs with grace.

Repentance unshackles us from pride and frees us for oneness.

THE PATH TO ONENESS

You knew it would come to this. We cannot avoid the "H" and the "S" words. Headship and submission are God's ordained means for achieving oneness in marriage. We're back to the ancient paths. But it's a good place to be. It really is. Don't be afraid to boldly take this path. It leads to God's best for marriage. The only dragon to be slain is pride. The journey takes us to the cross.

Headship is implied in Joshua's assertion that his household would serve the Lord. He speaks not just for himself but also for his family. Implied here is his wife's submission to his headship. He could not have made this declaration of family fealty if he had had a rebellious wife.

Biblical headship is humility in action. It is loving another more than self and putting the good of the other above self. If a man is motivated one whit by self-interest, he is not exercising leadership. He is practicing domination.

Submission has nothing to do with status or suppression. Men and women *are* equal. Submission has to do with function—the way God says the marriage is to work. Submission is not a legalistic list of behaviors. The wellspring of submission is humility before God and a heart that joyfully accepts familial order for the sake of God's glory.

If our home is to be a place of grace, we cannot exclude the marriage. No matter how much we love our children, they are not to be the centerpiece of the home. The substance and the sweetness of the gospel of grace must be applied to the marriage. Even if the recipient of this reflection of grace does not reciprocate, the aroma of grace can permeate the home.

What will headship and submission look like? The answer is easy. They will both look like Jesus. Ultimately these attitudes are about believing in a sovereign God who loves us beyond anything we can fathom and yielding to His plan.

The only thing that can unite two sinful creatures into one is the singular passion for God's glory. This passion is ignited by grace and fueled as we live in the realm of the covenant community, by the rubric of grace, and under the rule of covenant love.

A FINAL WORD

Lest you think that this emphasis on the realm, the rubric, and the rules of covenant marriage has nothing to do with the splendor and the sizzle of marriage, let me share the profound words of a friend of mine. Her sage advice to women: "We can be hot *and* holy."

In fact, I don't think you can separate the two.

THE ANCIENT PATH

Here is the ancient path, the good way. Meditate on it and pray that you will have the attitude of Christ.

> *Do nothing out of selfish ambition or vain conceit, but in humility consider others better than yourselves. Each of you should look not only to your own interests, but also to the interests of others.*
>
> *Your attitude should be the same as that of Christ Jesus: Who, being in very nature God, did not consider equality with God something to be grasped, but made himself nothing, taking the very nature of a servant, being made in human likeness. And being*

found in appearance as a man, he humbled himself and became obedient to death—even death on a cross!

Therefore God exalted him to the highest place and gave him the name that is above every name, that at the name of Jesus every knee should bow, in heaven and on earth and under the earth, and every tongue confess that Jesus Christ is Lord, to the glory of God the Father.

Therefore, my dear friends, as you have always obeyed—not only in my presence, but now much more in my absence—continue to work out your salvation with fear and trembling, for it is God who works in you to will and to act according to his good purpose. Do everything without complaining or arguing, so that you may become blameless and pure, children of God without fault in a crooked and depraved generation, in which you shine like stars in the universe as you hold out the word of life.

PHILIPPIANS 2:3-16

QUESTIONS AND ANSWERS

Q. My mate is not a Christian. Is our marriage a mistake?

A. No! Your marriage is not a mistake. God is sovereign, and "we know that in all things God works for the good of those who love him, who have been called according to his purpose" (Romans 8:28). We must bring the covenant of grace to bear upon the marriage that sovereign providence ordains for us.

Q. How can a man exercise headship without being tyrannical?

A. It's more about attitude than actions, but here are a few traps to avoid and suggestions to consider.

• A wife should not be treated as a child when it comes to decisions. Any man who makes unilateral decisions is acting foolishly. None of us sees the whole picture. Secure, mature leaders create an atmosphere in which those around them can have honest input. A wise man asks his wife for her opinion, respects her opinion, and asks if she feels the freedom to give her opinion. He values her feminine intuition and understands that it is not good for him to be alone in decision-making.

•A woman should not be held in financial bondage. She should have discretionary funds according to the family budget. To fail to trust her in this area demeans her.

•A man should be intentional in valuing his wife's contribution to the family. If she is a stay-at-home wife/mom, the world tells her that this is an insignificant role. She is shaping the character of children and providing the domestic support necessary for a husband to do his job. She needs encouragement and appreciation.

•Leadership communicates. A husband should tell his wife the real reason why he acts and reacts as he does. For example, when she mentions that she may make a purchase, sign a child up for soccer, invite friends over for dinner, or have a child's eyes examined, and he reacts negatively, she assumes that he does not care or does not trust her judgment. Often the problem is his concern about finances. He may feel that he is a failure because money is not available, and he does not want to admit this because of his fear of not providing. The failure is not in the area of finances. It is in the area of trust and communication.

•First and foremost, a man should pray with and for his wife, lead in family worship, and take responsibility to involve the family in corporate worship.

Q. Should a woman submit to her husband even when she does not agree with him?

A. Yes, but let me qualify this answer. A woman is not to submit to sin. If she is unsure whether something is a sin or a preference issue, she should ask the advice of a trusted, godly woman. Also, submission does not mean silence. When there is an area of disagreement, a woman needs to pray until she is sure she has released the issue at the cross. Then she needs to ask the Lord for wisdom to know whether she should express her opinion or remain silent. A woman can disagree with a submissive attitude. Once the decision is made, even if she disagrees and results prove him to be wrong, true submission jointly accepts the consequence and does not use it as a club.

BIBLE STUDY

1. Read the book of Ruth.
   - What characteristics of the covenant do you see? (These characteristics are listed in chapter 1.)
   - What do you learn from Ruth that is applicable to you?
   - What do you learn from Boaz?
   - What do you learn from Naomi's example?

2. Read Psalm 51, David's prayer of repentance, every day for a week. Then write your thoughts about this prayer.

3. Read Exodus 34:6-7. Pray for grace to glorify God by reflecting these characteristics of Him in your marriage.

4. Read Ephesians 5:21-33 again. Pray for grace to glorify God by obeying these commands.

5

Parenting

TELL THE NEXT GENERATION

Tom and Jane Patete, Atlanta, Georgia

Susan: *Tom and Jane, your home is a place of grace. Please share some of your pilgrimage with the next generation.*

Tom and Jane: *Not very fancy, even less expensive, sometimes a bit wobbly—that's the venue where much of our family's spiritual history unfolded. This kitchen table, the site of meals and a myriad of other gatherings, is an icon of the cumulative relationships, communication, and attempts at a Godward focus that contributed to our "corporate" growth in grace.*

More than just formal family worship, the teaching/learning events that took place here were primarily those that flow out of daily routines, both joys and sorrows, children's questions, life along the way. Experience was the backdrop for lessons on the deep things of God. To "think Christianly" was our goal, and be it by discipling or by discipline, to see the minds of children (indeed, of us all) gradually captured for Christ is the fruit to be cherished.

The round Formica-clad surface of this table also provided a comfort circle for visits by church members and neighbors alike. One particular ministry opportunity, recurring and still memorable, were the young wives/mothers seeking counsel. Among them, a single mom (whose life was a mess) stands out because together we navigated so many difficult trials with her. Troubles and problems were not always alleviated, and never easily, but the welcoming ambiance of a faith-based home supplied solace and a stage for teaching.

As varying portions of our extended family or other out-of-towners would come through our door, somehow the intimacy of the small table made it the center of fellowship. This perhaps gave us a natural ease in carrying on with those traditions that reflected the spiritual dimension of our home. On one such occasion, that pattern resulted in the husband of a visiting couple coming to terms with the Gospel he had heard many times previously—the witness that impacted him, quite to our amazement, was merely seeing a Christian family live as usual.

This so-called covenant table—a bit more wobbly now—continues today after more than three decades of uninterrupted use. Grandchildren now gather there to hear Bible stories, learn the catechism, and pray. Of special note is a comment by one of them in an early-morning conversation with Grandmom in which he observed that he needed to pray for a servant's heart. Seeing covenant kids develop as kingdom citizens is what it's all about!

My brethren, by all that is tender in the name of parents,
by all that is sacred in the vows of the covenant, by all that is interesting
in the riches of divine grace, by the value of our children as immortal beings,
by the joys of heaven and by the woes of hell, let us be incited, seriously
and earnestly, to attend to this subject, and bring up our children
in the nurture and admonition of the Lord.[1]

SAMUEL WORCESTER

*O*n a sermon preached in Salem, Massachusetts in 1811, Samuel Worcester said:

In all the relations of life, we need much of the grace of God in order to a fulfillment of the various duties of our relations; but scarcely in any relation do we need more of divine grace than in that of parents and heads of families. To have children committed to our care, to have immortal souls entrusted to our charge to be brought up for God and for everlasting glory in His kingdom, is certainly a situation of high responsibility, the duties of which cannot be fulfilled without great wisdom, diligence, and piety. Surely, my brethren, to discharge our duty to our children with fidelity, we must have a lively faith in the gracious promises of the covenant that, in giving them up to God in baptism, we may make an entire surrender of them; and that ever afterwards, in our prayers for them, and in all our counsels and instructions, we may be sincere and faithful, and have an unwavering reliance on Him for a blessing.

This faith which is necessary, in respect to our children, is not a vain confidence that the Lord will renew and save them whether we are faithful or not, but it is such a realizing view of His promise and faithfulness as will lead us constantly to look to Him, and humbly to depend upon Him, for all requisite grace. It is a faith which does honor to God, and gives all the glory of our salvation and the salvation of our children, to the riches of His mercy which, in His holy sovereignty, He has been pleased to reveal in His gracious covenant.[2]

Up to this point in Pastor Worcester's sermon, I am amening every word. But then he goes to meddling:

In proportion to our faith and piety, we shall be concerned for the salvation of our children, and shall be unceasing and abundant in our prayers, our instructions and admonitions, that they may be brought to renounce the vanities of the world and set their hope in God. But, my brethren, if we are not religious ourselves, how can we discharge our duty to our children? If we do not walk in our houses with a perfect heart, how can we command our children and our households after us to keep the way of the Lord? If we do not live habitually in the fear of the Lord, if we do not live, as the grace of God which brings salvation teaches, in the denial of ungodliness and worldly lusts, soberly, righteously, and devoutly in the world, how can we expect to train up our children in the way they should go, so that when they are old they will not depart from it? Oh, let us feel how important it is that we grow in grace and in the knowledge of our Lord and Savior, and be ever righteous before God, walking in all His statutes and ordinances blamelessly.[3]

Child-rearing is a highly charged topic—one that has been known to divide families and churches. Young parents land on a method and then cluster with others who have made the same choice. Lines are drawn. The culture of some churches is actually determined by the parenting method of choice of the majority of its members.

The methods and styles may be commendable, but one of my fears is that tightly structured systems may stunt our children's growth in the grace and knowledge of our Savior and His ways.

Another fear I have is that inappropriate reliance on systems can undermine the sanctification of parents. Systems can make us proud and arrogant. Covenant promises and requirements make us grateful and dependent. I am not saying we should not learn from methods and how-to books. What I am saying is that we should not be enslaved by them. Our starting point should be our theology; then we can select a variety of methods and ideas that will help us accomplish our overarching purpose.

As we examine Scripture, I am struck by the broad-stroke approach to parenting. There are actually relatively few specific instructions for parenting in the realm of the covenant. It seems to me that the covenantal model traditions a body of truth and a way of life based on that truth. This model cannot be programmed because it encompasses all of life. It is more about *who* we and our children are becoming than *what* we do. It is more about the life parents live before children than the rules we force them to keep.

Let me hasten to say that I am not suggesting that we compromise truth. Truth is absolute, and there is no wiggle room when it comes to the commands of God. But there is a difference between principle and preference, and there is room for variation on scheduling, bedtime, diet, method of discipline, and other issues of preference.

Another observation: As I reflect on what Scripture says about parenting in the realm of the covenant, I am stopped in my tracks. The scriptural admonitions probe the heart condition of the parent. God's Word exposes our sinfulness, drives us to the cross for mercy, and calls us to obedience. Pastor Worcester was right on the money—we will raise our children in a godly fashion in proportion to our own faith and piety.

Now let's consider some of the things Scripture tells us about our children and how to parent them. I pray that each principle will draw us to the cross for wisdom and grace.

PRINCIPLE 1: HEIRS OF THE PROMISE

After the resurrection and ascension of our Lord, Peter preached a stirring sermon to which the people responded: "'Brothers, what shall we do?' Peter replied, 'Repent and be baptized, every one of you, in the name of Jesus Christ for the forgiveness of your sins. And you will receive the gift of the Holy Spirit. The promise is for you and your children and for all who are far off—for all whom the Lord our God will call'" (Acts 2:37-39).

What promise? That Jewish congregation knew exactly what promise. They knew it was the covenant promise made to Abraham:

> *When Abram was ninety-nine years old, the LORD appeared to him. . . . Abram fell facedown, and God said to him, "As for me, this is my covenant with you: You will be the father of many nations. No longer will you be called Abram; your name will be Abraham, for I have made you a father of many nations. I will make you very fruitful; I will make nations of you, and kings will come from you. I will establish my covenant as an everlasting covenant between me and you and your descendants after you for the generations to come, to be your God and the God of your descendants after you."*
>
> GENESIS 17:1-7

But what does that have to do with us and our children? Paul answers in no uncertain terms: "If you belong to Christ, then you are Abraham's seed, and heirs according to the promise" (Galatians 3:29). The Old Testament physical kingdom of Israel foreshadows the New Testament spiritual kingdom. So the Old Testament life-perspective gives great insight for Abraham's seed on this side of the cross.

Clinging to God's covenant promise for our children is not an exercise in arrogance. It is not a denial of their sinfulness. Quite the opposite—it is an acknowledgment of their helpless condition and an unwavering trust in the promises of our covenant-keeping God as their only possible hope. Again let us listen to Pastor Worcester:

For about two thousand years, there were no churches, other than in families, and the cause of God was maintained in the world by means of family religion. And, since that period, both under the Mosaic and under the Christian dispensations, families have been distinctly recognized as constituent parts and nurseries of the Church. . . .

God's gracious and everlasting covenant with His church presents to believing parents a promise of spiritual and saving blessings to their children. The promise is to be a God to them and to their seed after them. For parents to take hold on this promise by faith, and looking to the Lord for the blessings which it contains for their children, is of high and eternal importance. It is only in the way of a dutiful reliance, indeed, on the covenant for all needed grace, that parents can bring up their children, as they are required to do, in the nurture and admonition of the Lord. This duty is to be performed in faith, and for the right performance of it, as of every other duty, parents certainly need abundant grace. . . . The grace promised in the covenant, to be received in a covenant way, is rich and sufficient. It is sufficient for parents, and it is sufficient for their children. It is sufficient to sanctify their hearts and to bring them to set their hope in God.

Were it not for the promises of the covenant, my brethren, would not believing parents sink under discouragements, and utterly despair of ever being able to train up their children for the holy service and kingdom of God? But in a believing reliance on these promises, have they not the greatest encouragement to be faithful in duty, and to hope that of His rich and covenanted mercy, God will in due time, make them to see that they have not labored in vain, but that they are the seed of the blessed of the Lord, and their offspring with them?[4]

I have a friend whose adult children are living as covenant breakers. She told me that each time a child is baptized in her church, her hope is renewed. She said, "I am reminded of God's faithfulness to His promise despite our children's unfaithfulness. I believe that in His time He will draw them to Himself, and I am reminded to pray more fervently that it might be so."

We often use the term "first-generation Christian" to refer to people who did not grow up in Christian homes. But I wonder if when we get to heaven, we will see that there was a believing grandmother or great-great-grandfather who prayed for the generations to come. Then we will see the realization of the mysterious wonder of the covenant promise running through families.

PUTTING PRINCIPLE 1 INTO PRACTICE

There are endless applications of each principle, but perhaps one example of each will help build the bridge from principle to practice.

Our children need to know they are heirs of the promise and that they live in the realm of the covenant. We can help them know they are valued members of this community by teaching them to value the family and the church. They should grow up hearing their parents pray for extended family members and for the church family. From the time they can talk, they can begin praying for their siblings, their cousins, their Sunday school teacher, and the pastor. Teach them the joy of hospitality as you plan family gatherings, have other church families in your home, and establish relationships with unbelieving neighbors through the ministry of hospitality. Teach them compassion by being compassionate. Tell your children why you are inviting the people who visited your church to dinner, taking the meal to the grieving family, or baby-sitting for the single mom.

Let your children help you. Let them pray with you that Jesus will use your efforts to show His love. In many families and church families there is competition and jealousy. Ask the Lord to rid your own heart of this sin and to replace this petty ugliness with a genuine joy in the blessings of others. Then nurture this selflessness in your children by reminding them that they are fellow heirs of the riches of God's grace.

Celebrate spiritual milestones. Have pull-out-all-the-stops celebrations for events such as a child ratifying the covenant by making his/her public profession of faith or the fiftieth anniversary of grandparents or a couple in your church.

PRINCIPLE 2: GIFTS FROM GOD

"Sons are a heritage from the LORD, children a reward from him" (Psalm 127:3). This is another Scripture that has been snatched from its context and reduced to calligraphy. There is nothing wrong with framed verses hanging in our homes, but let's be sure we don't miss the fullness of what they are saying.

Psalms 120-134 are known as the Songs of Ascents. These songs were sung by pilgrims as they made their way up to Jerusalem to worship. Imagine a village of believers walking together toward the Holy City, cooking and eating together around the campfires at night, singing the songs of Zion as they anticipate celebrating and worshiping together. These were community songs with several layers of meaning.

Read Psalm 127 and imagine that a father has been telling his children about the temple, the house of God. A group of men have been talking to a soon-to-be-married young man about building a family that will be a blessing in Israel. Some women have been sharing mothering tips with a young woman as they happily pass her baby from one to another. Then someone starts singing, and the others join in.

> *Unless the LORD builds the house, its builders labor in vain. Unless the LORD watches over the city, the watchmen stand guard in vain. In vain you rise early and stay up late, toiling for food to eat—for he grants sleep to those he loves. Sons are a heritage from the LORD, children a reward from him. Like arrows in the hands of a warrior are sons born in one's youth. Blessed is the man whose quiver is full of them. They will not be put to shame when they contend with their enemies in the gate.*
>
> PSALM 127:1-5

When they sing, "Sons are a heritage from the Lord, children a reward from him," the woman holding the baby sings the loudest because she knows there is something deeper than a biological connection. She has no biological children, but she spiritually mothers all the children in the village. This baby is a child of the covenant. He is a reward to the community. He is another sweet fulfillment of the promise to Abraham that they would become a mighty nation.

Our children are, indeed, gifts from the Lord. They are a sacred trust, not just to parents but to the kingdom. We must be good stewards of this treasure. We must shape them as a warrior shapes and stabilizes his arrows and then carefully aims them at the enemy.

Understanding the context of this psalm helped me to understand two portions of Scripture that previously puzzled me. For years I was in a quandary each time I read the account of Jesus' trip to Jerusalem with Mary and Joseph when he was twelve years old. Actually it was the return trip that baffled me. How could they possibly travel for a whole day before they realized their child had been left behind?

The problem was not them; it was me. I did not understand the covenant community perspective. Their perfectly reasonable assumption was that Jesus was safe because He was with their fellow pilgrims. I am not advocating that parents abandon their children to the care of others, but I am saying that I think we have lost this sense of community that gives parents assurance that we love their children as if they are our own, because they are.

My second dilemma was the episode when Jesus was teaching, and someone told him that His mother and brothers were outside. His response was surprising. "'Who are my mother and my brothers?' he asked. Then he looked at those seated in a circle around him and said, 'Here are my mother and my brothers! Whoever does God's will is my brother and sister and mother'" (Mark 3:33-35).

A covenant perspective helped me understand that Jesus was not ignoring His family. He was teaching us that grace runs deeper than blood. Grace relationships are for eternity. No Christian is homeless. We are a part of the family of God.

PUTTING PRINCIPLE 2 INTO PRACTICE

Whenever grandchildren spend the night with us, we have a bedtime ritual. I scratch their backs and "say verses." I recite some of the Scriptures I want embedded in their hearts and minds. Then I pray for each child, and I whisper, "You are a gift from the Lord to our family."

In our family we have lots of rituals. We have a growing number of "family verses" that the grands say together at family gatherings. We have motions for the verses, so it is a lively time. There are foods, traditions, stories, books, and conversations that are part of our family culture. Some—in fact most—are simple and silly, but they give us a sense of belonging and identity. I taught Hunter to tie his shoes, and since then we have had an ongoing conversation. I ask, "What did I do for you when you were little?" He responds, "You taught me to tie my shoes." I ask, "And what are you going to do for me?" He responds, "When you get really old, I'm going to tie your shoes." It's getting less silly as the years go by.

PRINCIPLE 3: TRAIN

"Train a child in the way he should go, and when he is old he will not turn from it" (Proverbs 22:6). Three words in this familiar verse fascinate me.

First word: Train. The Hebrew word for "train" is *hanak. The Theological Wordbook of the Old Testament* explains: "Although usually rendered 'dedicate,' a more accurate translation is 'begin' or 'initiate.' . . . *hanak* is almost certainly a community action."[5] In every place except Proverbs 22:6 the word is used in connection with structures such as a building or wall or altar.

Second word: A. I am also intrigued by the use of the singular rather than the plural. Even though *hanak* is "almost certainly a community action," the verse does not say, "Train *children* in the way *they* should go." This training demands a knowledge of each child's uniqueness and wisdom to find appropriate methods and styles.

Third word: Way. The context of Proverbs 22:6 is the rest of the book of Proverbs, part of the wisdom literature of the Old Testament. So this verse refers to the way of wisdom. According to *The Theological Wordbook of the Old Testament*, the essential idea of the wisdom writings of Scripture is

> a manner of thinking and attitude concerning life's experiences; including matters of general interest and basic morality. These concerns relate to prudence in secular affairs, skills in the arts, moral sensitivity, and experience in the ways of the Lord. . . . Reflected in OT wisdom is the teaching of a personal God who is holy and just and who expects those who know him to exhibit his character in the many practical affairs of life. . . . Therefore, Hebrew wisdom was not theoretical and speculative. It was practical, based on revealed principles of right and wrong, to be lived out in daily life. . . . The source of all wisdom is a personal God who is holy, righteous, and just.[6]

In no uncertain terms we are told that "the fear of the LORD is the beginning of wisdom, and knowledge of the Holy One is understanding" (Proverbs 9:10). The use of the name LORD, God's personal name most closely associated with the covenant, indicates that the way of wisdom is the way of covenant life among God's people.

Paul picks up on these ideas in his letter to the church in Ephesus: "Fathers, do not exasperate your children; instead, bring them up in the training and instruction of the Lord" (Ephesians 6:4). The word translated "training" is from the Greek word *paideia,* which means to train, discipline, chasten, and correct. *Instruction,* from the Greek *nouthesia,* involves admonition, instruction, and warning.

When we put it all together, we realize that we must study each child to discover how God has wired him/her. We must pray for wisdom to channel and expand those inclinations but not to cramp their style. I love spirited children. I love to see their eyes dance with excitement and their imaginations soar. A herd approach that stuffs all children into the same mold denies God's marvelous creativity in designing each child for the things He has purposed for him/her.

At the same time, there are boundaries. God's commands are not suggestions. There are consequences—indeed there are curses—for being covenant breakers. Children must be taught the way of wisdom in all relationships and endeavors; they must learn instant obedience to parents as preparation for wholehearted obedience to God, and there must be consequences for disobedience. This demands a recognition of their sinfulness and of God's mercy and grace to sinners.

PUTTING PRINCIPLE 3 INTO PRACTICE

Read the book of Proverbs often. Select a proverb each week to memorize during family worship. Make application of the verse to a child's or teen's life experiences. Our children grew up hearing Proverbs 15:1: "A gentle answer turns away wrath, but a harsh word stirs up anger," and Proverbs 20:11: "Even a child is known by his actions, by whether his conduct is pure and right." One of our family verses is Proverbs 3:5-6: "Trust in the LORD with all your heart and lean not on your own understanding; in all your ways acknowledge him, and he will make your paths straight."

Turn off the TV and read to your children. Biblical history is our family history, and covenant children should be well acquainted with these people and events. Read the classics. *Pilgrim's Progress* and The Chronicles of Narnia are our family favorites. At family gatherings we ask the children to plan a play based on a portion of one of these books, or we have one of them read a passage of Scripture while the others act it out. There have been some hilarious and memorable moments.

PRINCIPLE 4: SHOW AND TELL

The book of Deuteronomy is a family and a national survival manual. It is the record of Moses' farewell addresses to the Israelites before his death and their takeover of the promised land under the leadership of Joshua. They stood on the edge of this land inhabited by nations stronger and mightier than they, but Moses did not flinch. His message was full of hope based on the promises of God. He gave directions based on the commands of God. Consider this excerpt from Moses' magnum opus:

> *These are the commands, decrees and laws the LORD your God directed me to teach you to observe in the land that you are crossing the Jordan to possess, so that you, your children and their children after them may fear the LORD your God as long as you live by keeping all his decrees and commands that I give you, and so that you may enjoy long life.*
>
> *Hear, O Israel, and be careful to obey so that it may go well with you and that you may increase greatly in a land flowing with milk and honey, just as the LORD, the God of your fathers, promised you.*
>
> *Hear, O Israel: The LORD our God, the LORD is one. Love the LORD your God with all your heart and with all your soul and with all your strength. These commandments that I give you today are to be upon your hearts. Impress them on your children. Talk about them when you sit at home and when you walk along the road, when you lie down and when you get up. Tie them as symbols on your hands and bind them on your foreheads. Write them on the doorframes of your houses and on your gates. . . .*
>
> *In the future, when your son asks you, "What is the meaning of the stipulations, decrees and laws the LORD our God has commanded you?" tell him: "We were slaves of Pharaoh in Egypt, but the LORD brought us out of Egypt with a mighty hand. . . .*
>
> *"The LORD commanded us to obey all these decrees and to fear the LORD our God, so that we might always prosper and be kept alive, as is the case today."*
>
> DEUTERONOMY 6:1-9, 20-21, 24

God's people were to love the Lord with all their hearts. They were to obey His commands. Then they were to teach their children by word and deed to do the same. Nothing has changed.

Parents are commissioned to be the primary educators of their children. Regardless of the school option they choose, it is the parents who are accountable before God to steward the treasure entrusted to them. Teaching is more than passing on facts and figures. We are to teach a way of life based on the words of the one who said, "I am the way and the truth and the life" (John 14:6). We are to show and tell a biblical view of the world and of our place in that world.

The church is also responsible for teaching children. Psalm 78 is a call to the covenant community to tradition the faith to the next generation:

> *O my people, hear my teaching; listen to the words of my mouth. I will open my mouth in parables, I will utter hidden things, things from of old—what we have heard and known, what our fathers have told us. We will not hide them from their children; we will tell the next generation the praiseworthy deeds of the LORD, his power, and the wonders he has done. He decreed statutes for Jacob and established the law in Israel, which he commanded our forefathers to teach their children, so the next generation would know them, even the children yet to be born, and they in turn would tell their children. Then they would put their trust in God and would not forget his deeds but would keep his commands.*
>
> PSALM 78:1-7

The church is "the pillar and foundation of the truth" (1 Timothy 3:15), and believing parents have the unrivaled resource of the teaching and the relationships provided there. Louis Berkhof wrote:

> Now the children of the covenant are adopted into a family that is infinitely higher than the family of any man of rank or nobility. They are adopted into the family of the covenant God himself. Even while on earth they are privileged to join the company of the redeemed, the saints of God. They take their place in the church of Jesus Christ, which is the heavenly Jerusalem. Moreover, they are destined to live and move about eternally in the company of just men made perfect, of the innumerable hosts of the angels of God, and of Jesus Christ, the King all-glorious.

Perfect life in the most intimate communion with the tri-une God is their grand destiny; heaven with all its glories is their eternal home. Can we at all doubt whether this calls for Christian education? . . . Let us ever be mindful of the fact that the King's children must have a royal education.[7]

PUTTING PRINCIPLE 4 INTO PRACTICE

As we sit at home and walk along the way, our conversations should be "full of grace, seasoned with salt" (Colossians 4:6). We will hear *our* words and the tone of *our* speech come from the mouths of our children. The way you speak to a child is the way he/she will speak to a younger sibling. Do they hear the language of faith? Do they speak of the mercy and love of Jesus? Are they polite and gentle of speech? Listen to your children to hear yourself.

As we sit at home and walk along the way, one of the things we do most frequently is to sin against God and against one another. The need for repentance is constant. I am convinced that one of the most practical lessons we can teach our children is to ask God for grace to see their sin and for grace to repent. We need to teach them not to try to squirm out of taking responsibility for their wrongdoing. We need to teach them that to say, "I'm sorry *but* . . ." is no apology. It is blame-shifting. We must help them nurture their consciences and sense of justice more than their pride. How do we do this? Show and tell. Our children need to be taught the principle, but the degree to which they hear and apply it will be in direct proportion to the frequency they see it in the adults around them.

PRINCIPLE 5: WORSHIP

Every other principle stands or falls on this one. Worship is essential and central to holy living. True worship is not an event we attend at eleven o'clock on Sunday morning. It is a heart attitude that acknowl-edges God as the sovereign King who is worthy of our wholehearted obedience. It is an unambiguous loyalty to Him. It is a life that has been presented to God as "a living sacrifice, holy, acceptable to God" and that is not conformed to this world but is being transformed by the renewing of the mind (Romans 12:1-2). Worship is a way of life.

When children grow up in a family of faithful worshipers, they will see parents who honor the Sabbath, give their tithe, seek to glorify God in every relationship and decision, and go into their part of the world to tell others the wonders of God's grace. Then when these children ask, "What is the meaning of these things? Why do we live this way?" parents can reply, "Because we were slaves to the enemy of our souls, and the Lord delivered us into His kingdom. The Lord commanded us to live this way." This is the only way parents can ever say with integrity, "Because I say so." And there are times when that must be said, and it is all that can be said.

PUTTING PRINCIPLE 5 INTO PRACTICE

The Sabbath is the day of days for the child of God. Prepare for the Sabbath so that your children will sense that this is the high point of the week. Press the clothes on Saturday, be careful about Saturday night activities so that everyone is rested on Sunday, and use travel time to church to read Scripture and talk about the wonders of worship. Pray that your family will "give unto the LORD the glory due to His name" and will "worship the LORD in the beauty of holiness" (Psalm 29:2 NKJV).

Pray with your children that they will be an encouragement to others in your church family. Nurture this attitude by talking about how people encourage you. Help younger children participate in worship by marking their place in their Bible and in the hymnal. Find out early in the week what the hymns will be and practice them during family worship. Teach older children how to take notes during the sermon. Use mealtime after church for everyone to tell one thing they learned from the sermon or an encouragement they received from being with God's people.

Parents are sometimes thrown off track by unsound thinking that warns, "Don't force your faith on your children, or they will resent it. Don't make them go to church or participate in church activities." We never felt that our children had enough experience to make that decision. As long as their feet were under our table, they were expected to participate in church life. Too often parents fear their children's dislike more than they fear God's displeasure. We are covenant-bound to obey God's "stipulations, decrees and laws," and we are responsible to see that children under our care do the same. When children are resistant, we must pray for them, but we must not give in to them.

AN EXAMPLE

The story of Timothy is a sterling example of the covenantal model. It is a hopeful example because of the unexpected ingredient—his father was not a believer. None of our families is perfect. None of us has every piece in place. Yet God's grace is not constrained by our imperfections.

Timothy's mother was a believer, so he was an heir of the promise. His mother and grandmother were good stewards of this gift. They were women of sincere faith (2 Timothy 1:5) who faithfully taught Timothy the holy Scriptures from his infancy (3:15). The covenant community apparently assumed their responsibility to little Timothy. When Paul visited this community, "The brothers . . . spoke well of [Timothy]" (Acts 16:2). They spoke so well of Timothy that Paul invited the young man to join him in his missionary travels. I can picture it. The great apostle comes to town, and the men say, "Let us tell you about our boy Timothy. We've taught him the praiseworthy deeds of the Lord. We've instructed him in the way of wisdom. He's mature beyond his years. He's ready to be discipled by you."

Paul was a spiritual father to Timothy. He called Timothy a true son in the faith (1 Timothy 1:2). Paul made a huge investment in Timothy. Was it worth it? Consider his description of Timothy to the church in Philippi: "I hope in the Lord Jesus to send Timothy to you soon, that I also may be cheered when I receive news about you. I have no one else like him, who takes a genuine interest in your welfare. For everyone looks out for his own interests, not those of Jesus Christ. But you know that Timothy has proved himself, because as a son with his father he has served with me in the work of the gospel" (Philippians 2:19).

Timothy had a genuine interest in the welfare of others. He cared. He was not driven by self-interest but by kingdom interest. He was not concerned about recognition or reward. His desire was God's glory. He learned the way of wisdom and proved himself as he applied the knowledge of God to various situations and relationships. He had a servant's heart and a willingness to do the work of the Gospel.

No wonder Paul said, "I have no one else like him." Another translation says, "For I have no one like-minded" (NKJV). Another says, "For I have no one else of kindred spirit" (NASB). These few words declare the depth and richness of this relationship. These men had made the transition from a parent/child to a brotherly relationship. Paul did not keep Timothy in a dependent, subordinate position. They became soul buddies. They shared a singular purpose and passion—God's glory and the advancement of His kingdom.

Every parent should pray for wisdom to make this transition. We should be intentional in preparing for this shift. We should turn loose of the child and welcome the adult.

Timothys should not be the exception in the covenant community. Timothys are what we can expect when parents, grandparents, and covenant communities pray and work together to teach the holy Scriptures and to show the way of wisdom. Paul saw the results of this kind of investment, and he challenged Timothy to the same kind of ministry: "You then, my son, be strong in the grace that is in Christ Jesus. And the things you have heard me say in the presence of many witnesses entrust to reliable men who will also be qualified to teach others" (2 Timothy 2:1-2). This is our calling and our challenge.

A CAUTION

Timothys are what we should pray for and expect, but we must be careful not to drift into the trap of "if I do A, God will do B." It is very easy to be ambushed by that kind of legalistic, performance-oriented thinking. As soon as our children's outcome becomes our motive, we are trapped. Our sights must be on God's glory.

From our perspective, life often does not make sense and does not seem good. We see faithful parents whose children turn from the faith. We see unfaithful parents whose children embrace the faith. There are loving parents whose children die. There are young Timothys in our churches who are killed. But this we know—God is good, and what He does is good.

THE ANCIENT PATH

Here is the ancient path, the good way. Meditate on it and pray this Scripture for your children, grandchildren, and the children in your church.

> *For this reason I kneel before the Father, from whom his whole family in heaven and on earth derives its name. I pray that out of his glorious riches he may strengthen you with power through his Spirit in your inner being, so that Christ may dwell in your hearts through faith. And I pray that you, being rooted and established in love, may have power, together with all the saints, to grasp how wide and long and high and deep is the love of Christ, and to know this love that surpasses knowledge—that you may be filled to the measure of all the fullness of God.*
> EPHESIANS 3:14-19

I have prayed this passage for our children for years, and now I pray it for our grandchildren. If children begin to comprehend the expanse of God's love, they will be compelled to live for His glory. We can think big thoughts and pray big prayers for our children because we have a God "who is able to do immeasurably more than all we ask or imagine, according to his power that is at work within us, to him be glory in the church and in Christ Jesus throughout all generations, for ever and ever! Amen" (vv. 20-21).

QUESTIONS AND ANSWERS

Q. *I understand that there are no formulas, but how do we decide methods of discipline, or bedtimes, or curfews for our teens, and other specific day-to-day issues? Is it wrong to read the how-to books?*

A. No! Read the books and attend the seminars, but remember that you must adapt the ideas to your family and your child. Some suggestions regarding dealing with specifics:

First, pray. Parenting requires the pray-without-ceasing kind of praying. Just about the time you learn how to parent one age, the child grows out of it. And much of what you learn with one child does not apply to the next child.

Second, learn from the experts, but always remember that they do not know your family and your child. You must adapt and apply.

Third, find two or three people who are farther along the parenting pathway than you are and who know and love the Lord and who know and love you and your child. They may be your parents, grandparents, or people in your church. Give them permission to give you advice. Tell them in advance that you want to listen to several perspectives before you make your decision.

Fourth, pray for wisdom. God has given that child to you, and you are the ones to whom He will give the wisdom and the grace to parent that child. The blend of your perspectives gives balance to your parenting. Don't underestimate your sanctified common sense. And for the single parent, ask the Lord to supply that balance you need.

A word to the person who is asked to *give* advice: When a young parent gives you permission to give advice, you should give them permission not to take your advice. Always remind them that *they* are the parents whom God has entrusted with that child.

Fifth, relax and enjoy your child. We have one grandchild who entered the world determined to examine and conquer it. Her mother found her in bizarre places before anyone thought she could get to those places. Recently I was looking at some baby pictures of her. There was one of her sitting in front of the open door of the refrigerator with food on the floor all around her. There was another of her with her mother's makeup scattered around her and her face covered with lipstick. In both she was grinning with delight. When I asked her mother about the pictures, her response was classic: "That's when I decided to stop fighting it and take pictures. I knew the time would come when we would laugh about her escapades."

BIBLE STUDY

1. Read the book of Proverbs and make a list of verses you want your family to memorize during the next year. You may want to select one for each week or one for each month. Write the first ones on index cards and put them on your refrigerator, in the car, and with your family devotional material.

2. Read Exodus 34:6-7. Pray for grace to reflect these characteristics to your children.

3. Read Deuteronomy 6-8.
    • What do you learn about God?
    • What parental and community responsibilities are given?
    • What warnings are given?
    • What promises are given?

4. Read Deuteronomy 29-30, the covenant renewal at Moab. Write a prayer of covenant renewal based on this passage.

6

Resources

TELL THE NEXT GENERATION

Joel and Carol Esther Belz, Asheville, North Carolina

Susan: *Joel and Carol Esther, many of us learned from you about the importance of not withdrawing from the covenant community during times of family crisis. Will you tell the next generation how to utilize the resources of God's church when the enemy is assaulting our families?*

Joel and Carol Esther: *"Can you imagine the fear and pain of not knowing where your child is?" asked a woman requesting prayer for a family whose son was missing.*

Well, yes, I could. "But," I said, "the pain that's worse is to know where your child is—and have something worse than your worst fears confirmed."

We thought we had already passed God's test of giving up a child. When our youngest daughter Esther, only eight days old, was hospitalized to be tested for fatal diseases, we waited and prayed for three days. She was His, but He blessed us with her recovery. Now Esther was one of the many standing with us in prayer for her next older sister Elizabeth, who was in much greater danger—the danger of falling into the hands of the living God due to pursuing her own will. That pursuit had led to her excommunication from the church.

Among all the lessons God had for us to learn, none was more important than how we needed to be supported by the prayers of the church—and how that body needed also to be called upon. This trial was not ours alone. It belonged to the body. *Our trial was part of the larger picture of what God was purposing for good in many lives.*

So there was hardly a time when Covenant Reformed Presbyterian Church people were gathered that Elizabeth was not prayed for aloud, often with a broken voice. Elders prayed from the pulpit on Sunday mornings, women at their Tuesday morning Bible studies, and everyone on Wednesday evenings. And we knew that even when we were not present in homes of church families, they prayed.

But the body is not limited to one local congregation. As God's people learned of the evil one's kidnapping of one of God's sheep, they joined us in prayer all over the world. In England, France, Africa, India, Asia, Mexico, Honduras, and Chile people prayed. Today I have as a treasured possession a basketful of notes and cards representing prayers offered up to our faithful Father that He would be pleased to number Elizabeth among His own.

Without such agonizing and faithful prayer by the larger body, how could they possibly have known—and shared—the fullness of our joy when Elizabeth was at last reinstated as a member of the church at a Communion service, with all her sisters present? Following our pastor's lead in kneeling before the Lord to give thanks to the Father, we all knew together how each of us had been rescued from the dominion of darkness and brought into the kingdom of the Son He loves.

Earnest, secret, believing prayer should never cease to be daily
presented for our offspring. . . . Daily we should wrestle with God for
their eternal salvation. . . . That parent has neglected a very important branch
of his duty, who has suffered one single day to pass by without bearing
his children upon his heart before God in private prayer.[1]

JOHN ANGELL JAMES

*I*t is staggering to think that God would entrust the institution of
marriage, a union that is to illustrate the relationship between Christ and
the church, to sinful creatures. It is amazing that He would give the
monumental task of child-rearing to novices. And consider the fact that
God clumps what looks like an improbable combination of people
together and calls us His body. The fact that families survive and thrive
and that His kingdom advances is surely a work of grace and mercy.

Let's be candid. Doing family God's way is not the easy way. It's
downright hard. In fact, it's war. It's a holy war for the soul of the family. Soldiering is not for the slothful. Advancing Christendom family
by family is for those ablaze with passion for God's glory. It is the way
of denial of self. It is the way of service. Dr. Edward Payson wrote,
"This world is the place for labor, and not for rest or enjoyment,
except that enjoyment which may be found in serving God. We shall
have time enough in the coming world to rest and to converse with
our friends; and it may well reconcile us to separation here, if we hope
to be forever with them there."[2]

For Abraham, doing family God's way meant being willing to sacrifice his son (Genesis 22). For Hannah, it meant being willing to give
her son to God's service (1 Samuel 1). For Mary, mothering the
Messiah meant a sword in her soul (Luke 2:34-35). But God gave
them what He promises to all His children: "My grace is sufficient for
you, for my power is made perfect in weakness" (2 Corinthians 12:9).

Is that grace an ethereal otherworldly kind of thing that sounds wonderful but doesn't really help me when the kids are cranky, the pot roast is burned, and the battery in my car is dead? What resources does God give me when things are spinning out of control, and I feel I may go over the edge and never come back? Nothing new here— our resources are the same as those that God has provided for His children through the ages:

- His Word
- His Spirit
- Prayer
- The church

God still tells us to "stand at the crossroads and look; ask for the ancient paths, ask where the good way is, and walk in it, and you will find rest for your souls" (Jeremiah 6:16).

These resources draw us to the Lord and to His people, so they fortify us against an individualistic perspective of family.

These resources empower us to live beyond our own ability. They move us to the grace zone so that we can glorify God by reflecting His goodness to others.

These resources teach us how to live in the realm of the covenant, according to the rubric of grace and by the rule of love.

These resources equip us for oneness in our marriages and maturity in our parenting.

These resources guide us to cultivate havens of grace that are a preview of our heavenly home.

These resources transcend time and place.

They point us to the God who simultaneously transcends time and place and intimately enters time and place so that His children can live in His presence and reflect His glory, regardless of their time and place.

GOD'S WORD

We know that God's Word is the Christian's resource, but do we really know it? Do we comprehend the magnitude of this gift? Do we resonate with the reality that "the word of our God stands forever" (Isaiah 40:8), that it *will* accomplish His purpose (Isaiah 55:11) because it is "living and active" and so sharp that "it penetrates even to dividing soul and spirit, joints and marrow; it judges the thoughts and attitudes of the heart" (Hebrews 4:12)?

Do we understand in the depths of our souls that His Word is flawless (Proverbs 30:5) and eternal (Psalm 119:89)?

There is such a thing as absolute truth, and it has actually been entrusted to the followers of the Most High God. Our Savior knew the power and practicality of this resource, so He prayed, "Sanctify them by the truth; your word is truth" (John 17:17).

God does not send His warriors into battle without a superior weapon. We are armed with "the sword of the Spirit, which is the word of God" (Ephesians 6:17).

Diligent study and determined application of God's Word must be a priority for the child of God.

GOD'S SPIRIT

When Jesus accomplished the work of our redemption and returned to heaven, He did not leave us to decipher the gift of His Word on our own. "As a father has compassion on his children, so the LORD has compassion on those who fear him; for he knows how we are formed, he remembers that we are dust" (Psalm 103:13-14). So He left His Spirit to teach, guide, and comfort us. "But the Counselor, the Holy Spirit, whom the Father will send in my name, will teach you all things and will remind you of everything I have said to you" (John 14:26).

His Spirit empowers us. "But you will receive power when the Holy Spirit comes on you; and you will be my witnesses in Jerusalem, and in all Judea and Samaria, and to the ends of the earth" (Acts 1:8).

This power is reminiscent of the fire that came upon Mt. Sinai when God gave His people the law, but that time they fled because they could not bear the sight of it. They begged Moses to serve as go-between. At Pentecost something different happened. Their Mediator had mediated so the fire could come upon them without consuming them. "They saw what seemed to be tongues of fire that separated and came to rest on each of them" (Acts 2:3).

This fire cleansed and empowered them so that they became the very temple of the Holy Spirit. And this inheritance is given to every child of God. "Do you not know that your body is a temple of the Holy Spirit, who is in you, whom you have received from God?" (1 Corinthians 6:19).

Paul calls this energy God's "incomparably great power for us who believe. That power is like the working of his mighty strength, which he exerted in Christ when he raised him from the dead and seated him at his right hand in the heavenly realms" (Ephesians 1:19-20). Think about this! The very power that was applied to raise Jesus from the dead is available to us.

This is the power that produces God's character in us. "But the fruit of the Spirit is love, joy, peace, patience, kindness, goodness, faithfulness, gentleness and self-control" (Galatians 5:22-23). A home where this fruit is in abundance is surely a place of grace.

PRAYER

Our resources are phenomenal. We actually have access to God. "Therefore, brothers, since we have confidence to enter the Most Holy Place by the blood of Jesus, let us draw near to God with a sincere heart in full assurance of faith . . ." (Hebrews 10:19, 22).

The Lord of the universe says to "call to me and I will answer you and tell you great and unsearchable things you do not know" (Jeremiah 33:3). And He says that the "prayer of a righteous man is powerful and effective" (James 5:16).

We know this in our heads, but so often we try every other self-effort solution before we cast ourselves before Him and ask for help.

THE CHURCH

God supplies His church with gifts that are to be used for the mutual good of His family. The Westminster Confession of Faith explains that those who are united to Christ are "united to one another in love, they have communion in each other's gifts and graces, and are obliged" to share them for the "mutual good, both in the inward and outward man."[3]

Some of those gifts and graces are life experiences of older members that can help young parents bring their children up in the nurture and admonition of the Lord. Paul challenged Titus to equip older women so they could teach younger women how to love their husbands and children. Paul spiritually fathered Timothy and challenged Timothy to do the same for others.

There are the gifts and graces of preaching, teaching, praying, encouraging, leading, serving, and helping. No parents should engage in the battle for the hearts and minds of their children apart from this resource. No child of God should live apart from this resource. Community worship is one of the themes of Psalm 68. In that context we read that God is a "father to the fatherless, a defender of widows" and that He "sets the lonely in families" (Psalm 68:5-6). The work and worship of the community is the haven for the vulnerable and lonely. Sixteen year-old Avy understands this. She writes:

> I am one of seven children. I experienced firsthand God's love and mercy through the women at our church. My family went through a crisis when it was unsafe for us to stay at our house. My mother talked with one of the ladies in the church, and she asked my mom for permission to share the situation with our pastor. Then, without hesitation, she opened her home to us. We stayed there for a week until a shelter was available.
>
> The night we were to move to the shelter, my mom's Bible study group came and helped us. That evening was a night to remember. My youngest sister locked herself in the bathroom. The fire department had to come and rescue her with a ladder to the second-story window. The women took this in stride and encouraged the rest of us not to worry and to eat our dinner. They brought dinner for twelve.

Someone made our lunches for school the next day. They helped us pack, moved us in their cars, and helped us settle in at the shelter.

During this troubling period for our family, the women in our church showed us God's love and support. At Christmas God sent these women to remind us of the birth of Christ and the joy He brought. I watched as God used ordinary people to give to us extraordinary love and compassion. One woman made Christmas stockings for each of us, and the women of the church filled those stockings.

I want to learn to give the same compassion to my fellow brothers and sisters and to share with others what God has done for me. I want to walk with these women in the footsteps of Christ.

Does this mean that the church will always behave well and present a faithful witness to our children as Avy's church did for her? We must pray so, but we know it will not always be so on this side of glory. Those times when church members disappoint us and disgrace the faith are times for others to pray and forgive. Perhaps our response is what our children really need to see. As imperfect as the church is, God says that those who are planted in it will thrive: "The righteous will flourish like a palm tree, they will grow like a cedar of Lebanon; planted in the house of the LORD, they will flourish in the courts of our God. They will still bear fruit in old age, they will stay fresh and green, proclaiming, 'The LORD is upright; he is my Rock, and there is no wickedness in him'" (Psalm 92:12-15).

UTILIZING THE RESOURCES

King Jehoshaphat had his ups and downs. Don't we all? I think he peaked when the Moabites, Ammonites, and Meunites came to make war on him. Let me encourage you to put this book down and pick up the Book. Read 2 Chronicles 20, and then get back to me.

Did you notice that when Jehoshaphat heard about the vast army, he was alarmed. He should have been. He was responsible for a kingdom of people. We can learn from Jehoshaphat. We should be alarmed about the vast army of paganism, relativism, materialism, and secularism assaulting the family. Many Christians are anesthetized into complacency. Wise parents, grandparents, and church leaders recognize the enemy.

Jehoshaphat's alarm took him exactly where our sanctified sensibilities about the culture wars should take us. He "resolved to inquire of the LORD, and he proclaimed a fast for all Judah." He was not paralyzed by naivete or fear. He listened to the reports, identified the enemy, and began utilizing his resources.

He employed the resources of prayer and of the covenant community. He was not afraid to risk his position of leadership by admitting his need. He called people from every town in Judah to come together to "seek help from the LORD."

Jehoshaphat knew the transcendent character of God. He stood before all the people and said, "O LORD, God of our fathers, are you not the God who is in heaven? You rule over all the kingdoms of the nations. Power and might are in your hand, and no one can withstand you" (2 Chronicles 20:6).

Jehoshaphat *acted* covenantally by calling the people together, and then he *spoke* covenantally: "O our God, did you not drive out the inhabitants of this land before your people Israel and give it forever to the descendants of Abraham your friend?" (v. 7). With these words, Jehoshaphat reminded the people to *think* covenantally. His leadership is stunning.

Then Jehoshaphat prayed the bottom-line prayer that we all must pray when we face a vast army: "O our God, will you not judge them? For we have no power to face this vast army that is attacking us. We do not know what to do, but our eyes are upon you" (v. 12).

Following Jehoshaphat's lead, "All the men of Judah, with their wives and children and little ones, stood there before the LORD" (v. 13). This is leadership—leading men, women, and children to stand before the Lord. Jehoshaphat got out of the way in order to show the way. The result?

Then the Spirit of the LORD came upon Jahaziel. . . . He said: "Listen, King Jehoshaphat and all who live in Judah and Jerusalem! This is what the LORD says to you: 'Do not be afraid or discouraged because of this vast army. For the battle is not yours, but God's. Tomorrow march down against them. . . . You will not have to fight this battle. Take up your positions; stand firm and see the deliverance the LORD will give you, O Judah and Jerusalem. Do not be afraid; do not be discouraged. Go out to face them tomorrow, and the LORD will be with you.'"

2 CHRONICLES 20:14-17

Jehoshaphat's leadership did not stifle God's work in others. He did not have to be on center stage. Note his response to Jahaziel's encouragement: "Jehoshaphat bowed with his face to the ground, and all the people of Judah and Jerusalem fell down in worship before the LORD" (v. 18).

There was unity of purpose as the covenant community worshiped.

Jehoshaphat utilized the resource of God's Word as he reminded the people of God's faithfulness: "Listen to me, Judah and people of Jerusalem! Have faith in the LORD your God and you will be upheld; have faith in his prophets and you will be successful" (v. 20).

Then he consulted the people, and together they decided on what appears to be a reckless strategy. "Jehoshaphat appointed men to sing to the LORD and to praise him for the splendor of his holiness as they went out at the head of the army, saying: "Give thanks to the LORD, for his love endures forever" (v. 21). It was bold, but it was not reckless. They knew exactly what they were doing. They sang the song that had been sung when Solomon dedicated the temple.

The trumpeters and singers joined in unison, as with one voice, to give praise and thanks to the LORD. Accompanied by trumpets, cymbals and other instruments, they raised their voices in praise to the LORD and sang: "He is good; his love endures forever." Then the temple of the LORD was filled with a cloud, and the priests could not perform their service because of the cloud, for the glory of the LORD filled the temple of God.

2 CHRONICLES 5:13-14

Our Creator and Redeemer is good. His covenant love for His covenant people endures forever. This is the song of the covenant that celebrates the God of the covenant. When this song was sung at the dedication, the temple was filled with the glory of the Lord. God's temple today—you and I—is filled with His glory when our hearts burst with the song of the covenant: "He is good; His love endures forever."

His Word and His Spirit, prayer, and the fellowship of the body are His resources to draw us to His presence. It is His presence that distinguishes our family from every other family on the face of the earth. He has given every resource we need to build homes that are places of grace because they reflect the character of the God of grace.

Those resources were sufficient for Jehoshaphat's army. "As they began to sing and praise, the LORD set ambushes against the men of Ammon and Moab and Mount Seir . . ." (v. 22). Infighting began, and these armies annihilated each other. "When the men of Judah came to the place that overlooks the desert and looked toward the vast army, they saw only dead bodies lying on the ground; no one had escaped" (v. 24).

It took Jehoshaphat and his men three days to collect all of the plunder.

On the fourth day they assembled in the Valley of Beracah, where they praised the LORD. . . . Then, led by Jehoshaphat, all the men of Judah and Jerusalem returned joyfully to Jerusalem, for the LORD had given them cause to rejoice over their enemies. They entered Jerusalem and went to the temple of the LORD with harps and lutes and trumpets. The fear of God came upon all the kingdoms of the countries when they heard how the LORD had fought

*against the enemies of Israel. And the kingdom of Jehoshaphat was
at peace, for his God had given him rest on every side.*

2 CHRONICLES 20:26-30

Families face vast armies, but when we follow Jehoshaphat's strategy and utilize the resources God provides, God will fight the battles for us, and we will gather the blessings.

It's hard for fearful, naïve people to admit there is an enemy. "Things aren't so bad. Our kids know what's right. They'll be fine."

It's hard for prideful, self-sufficient people to admit they need the Lord and each other. "We can handle this. We'll work it out. No one at church needs to know about it."

It's hard for all of us to stand before the Lord and wait when we hear the sound of the vast army and feel the enemy's arrows whizzing by our heads. We begin thinking our situation is beyond hope. Have I got a story for you!

DRY BONES

I can think of nothing as lifeless as dry bones, and yet that is the very imagery God uses in Ezekiel 37 to teach us that nothing is too dead for Him. Whether it is a dead marriage, the temper tantrums of a toddler, the rebelliousness of a teen, an unbelieving adult child, or a financial black hole, if you feel that you are in the middle of a valley of dry bones—read on.

> *The hand of the LORD was upon me, and he brought me out by the Spirit of the LORD and set me in the middle of a valley; it was full of bones. He led me back and forth among them, and I saw a great many bones on the floor of the valley, bones that were very dry. He asked me, "Son of man, can these bones live?" I said, "O Sovereign LORD, you alone know."*

I must admit that my response would have been different. I would have been sure that I could answer this question, and my answer would have been "NO!" Ezekiel's faith-response positioned him to see something extraordinary. What an understatement.

Then he said to me, "Prophesy to these bones and say to them, 'Dry bones, hear the word of the LORD! This is what the Sovereign LORD says to these bones: I will make breath enter you, and you will come to life. I will attach tendons to you and make flesh come upon you and cover you with skin; I will put breath in you, and you will come to life. Then you will know that I am the LORD.'"

EZEKIEL 37:4-6

Can you imagine standing in the middle of a basin of bones and being told to preach to them? Even if you agreed to tell the bones that they would come to life, can you imagine believing it would happen? Ezekiel believed the unbelievable.

So I prophesied as I was commanded. And as I was prophesying, there was a noise, a rattling sound, and the bones came together, bone to bone. I looked, and tendons and flesh appeared on them and skin covered them, but there was no breath in them. Then he said to me, "Prophesy to the breath; prophesy, son of man, and say to it, 'This is what the Sovereign Lord says: Come from the four winds, O breath, and breathe into these slain, that they may live.'" So I prophesied as he commanded me, and breath entered them; they came to life and stood up on their feet—a vast army.

EZEKIEL 37:7-10

Here is another vast army, and this time it is not the enemy.

Then he said to me: "Son of man, these bones are the whole house of Israel. They say, 'Our bones are dried up and our hope is gone; we are cut off.' Therefore prophesy and say to them: 'This is what the Sovereign LORD says: O my people, I am going to open your graves and bring you up from them; I will bring you back to the land of Israel. Then you, my people, will know that I am the LORD, when I open your graves and bring you up from them.'"

EZEKIEL 37:11-13

We are often in the middle of people and circumstances that are as dead as dry bones. They have absolutely no ability to rise up and rattle themselves together. They cannot cover themselves with flesh. Our hope for them is not in their ability.

> *"'I will put my Spirit in you and you will live, and I will settle you in your own land. Then you will know that I the LORD have spoken, and I have done it, declares the LORD.'"*
>
> EZEKIEL 37:14

For people and situations that are lifeless, the only reasonable resources are those provided by the Lord God. These resources move us beyond what is seen to the unseen real. These resources enable us to see the vast army at our disposal. When the king of Aram sent his army to capture Elisha, they surrounded the city. Elisha's servant panicked. "What should we do?" he cried.

> *"Don't be afraid," the prophet answered. "Those who are with us are more than those who are with them." And Elisha prayed, "O LORD, open his eyes so he may see." Then the LORD opened the servant's eyes, and he looked and saw the hills full of horses and chariots of fire all around Elisha.*
>
> 2 KINGS 6:16-17

Ask God to open your spiritual eyes that you may see. He has given all we need. His Word, His Spirit, prayer, and the church are part of our inheritance. We must not squander this wealth.

THE ANCIENT PATH

Here is the ancient path, the good way. Meditate on it. Memorize Psalm 100 with your family. If there are younger children, make up motions. Pray this psalm into the life of your children, grandchildren, and the children in your church.

Make a joyful shout to the LORD, all you lands!
Serve the LORD with gladness; Come before His presence
with singing. Know that the LORD, He is God; It is He who
has made us, and not we ourselves; We are His people and the
sheep of His pasture. Enter into His gates with thanksgiving, and
into His courts with praise. Be thankful to Him, and bless His
name. For the LORD is good; His mercy is everlasting, and His
truth endures to all generations (NKJV).

QUESTIONS AND ANSWERS

Q. Our life seems to be in a frenzy. We are going in so many directions,
and everyone is so busy. How can we utilize these resources in a regular, con-
sistent way?

A. First, take a prayerful look at your family's schedule. You may
need a radical strategy. Jehoshaphat's strategy of putting the musicians
at the front of his army was bizarre from a military viewpoint.
Adjusting your family life to the rubric of the covenant may require
extreme measures. Or you may need to make a simple adjustment
such as limiting TV viewing and making better use of your time. You
might ask an older person or couple to observe your family life and
to give you their perspective. Then take it one step at a time. Don't
try to rearrange your entire life in one day.

Busy isn't necessarily bad. Are you busy with worthwhile things,
or is there a lot of wasted time? Simply being intentional with your
time can redeem many minutes. Are you utilizing driving time to
memorize Scripture with your children or waiting-for-the-child-
taking-piano-lessons time to pray for your family or read to another
child?

Utilizing these resources is a way of life. Remember that creating a godly family is more about attitude than schedules. These kingdom benefits are to be woven into the fabric of how we live. It is not
just scheduling family worship, as important as that is. It is attaching
all we do to what we believe.

John Angell James wrote about teaching our children through
the education of circumstances:

It is the sentiments you let drop occasionally, it is the conversation they overhear, when playing in the corner of the room, which has more effect than many things which are addressed to them directly. . . . Your example will educate them—your conversation with your friends—the business they see you transact—the likings and dislikings you express—these will educate them. . . . The education of circumstances . . . is of more constant and powerful effect, and of far more consequence to the habit, than that which is direct and apparent. This education goes on at every instant of time; it goes on like time—you can neither stop it nor turn its course.[4]

Q. I know the teaching our family receives at church is important, but I never thought about the people being a resource. How do we tap into this?
A. First, be a resource to others. Get involved in serving, whether it is on a clean-up committee or a visitation committee. Get involved as a family by finding some ways you can serve together. Then invite people into your life. Go for picnics with other families; get together with other parents to pray for your children; offer to help those in crisis and be willing to ask for help when you need it.
Q. Isn't this risky? Can I really trust others?
A. Yes, it is risky. The more you love other people, the greater the potential to be hurt or disappointed by them. No one but Jesus is totally trustworthy, but He has told us to love, serve, encourage, help, and pray for each other. This also means being willing to receive those graces from others.

One way we can minimize the risk is by guarding our relationships with prayer. When people pray with and for one another, they put a wall of protection around that relationship.

BIBLE STUDY

1. Read 2 Chronicles 20.
   • What do you learn about God?
   • What vast army are you facing?

- As you face the vast army, how are you utilizing the resources at your disposal?

2. Read:
   - Ezekiel 34:11-16, 25-31
   - Ezekiel 36:24-28
   - Ezekiel 37

3. Read Psalm 92 every day for a week.

PART TWO

Gazing at Glory

A few days after Annie Grace died, my Bible reading was Acts 7. As I read about the stoning of Stephen, I identified in a way I had never experienced before. Stones of grief were ripping my soul open. It was as if I understood what Stephen endured. I also read of Stephen's response with a new level of understanding. "But he, being full of the Holy Spirit, gazed into heaven and saw the glory of God, and Jesus standing at the right hand of God, and said, 'Look! I see the heavens opened and the Son of Man standing at the right hand of God!'" (Acts 7:55-56 NKJV). The stones continued to pelt his body, but Stephen gazed at glory, and he saw Jesus. I knew that I had to gaze at glory, regardless of the weight or duration of the stones of grief. Over the next weeks I gazed hard, and in God's Word I saw His glory.

Sometimes life is hard. Sometimes it is painful. The stones of life assail our families and us. I could do nothing to fix our daughter's pain over the death of her child. I can't shield you from the stones being hurled at you. I can only tell you what I learned when I gazed at glory. I pray that it will help you gaze at glory. I think this is the way we can build homes that are places of grace.

7

The Glorious One

TELL THE NEXT GENERATION

Chuck and Sharon Betters, Bear, Delaware

Susan: *Chuck and Sharon, I love the way you are parenting your adult children and their families. You seem to have made the transition from children to friends. I know this did not just happen. Tell us some of the things you do to make your adult children comfortable being your friends.*

Chuck and Sharon: *Friendship with our adult children is not so different from the friendship we experienced when they were little. And it's not so different from our friendship with others. From the time our children were born, we intentionally created a safe place in which they could mature and observe intimacy with Christ. We were not shocked when they sinned, and we encouraged them to fail forward. We wanted them to fail in front of us so that we could teach them not only about consequences for bad behavior but about grace. Sometimes when we observed genuine repentance, we lifted the discipline earlier than they expected and explained that our grace was a reflection of God's grace toward us. Our son Chuck replied to your question, "I can talk to my dad about any problem, and rather than condemning me when I've made a mistake, he teaches me how to make it right or how to honestly face temptation. I'm not afraid to talk to him about anything."*

True friendship requires respect, and that doesn't just happen when the children turn eighteen. Genuinely listening and hearing, not only words but also the heart of the speaker, communicates respect even to a little child. As long as the children's words reflected respect for us and our wisdom, we engaged in dis-

cussions that were sometimes heated. As they matured, those discussions have transitioned from ending with our words, "That's my decision!" to, "This is our opinion, but we will respect whatever decision you make."

The long car trips to and from school and activities were especially important times to ask specific questions to generate discussions about activities and friendships. Our open bedroom door was an invitation for them to "report in" after evening activities. Our daughter Heidi remembers long late-night conversations as she sprawled across our bed until we fell asleep. Our son Dan said, "There is always an open line of communication between us now, because there always has been since I can remember. My parents push me, but they are not pushy. They are giving, but not spoiling. They instruct, but are not overbearing." Shortly before our son Mark's death, Mark wrote to his dad, "Any question that I ask you, you have never failed to answer; any problem that I bring to you, you never failed to help me through."

True friendship requires encouragement. We always try to find something good to say about every situation, no matter how bleak.

As our children have left our home to build extensions of our family, we have assured them that they are still safe with us. They know we will not have any negative discussions about them with their siblings or anyone else. And they know we want them to stay close to us. We don't wait for them to make the first move—we regularly call them just to talk. We often ask if their children can come over to play, even if they don't need a baby-sitter.

Friendship requires feeling important to the other person. Our kids and our congregation knew that our ministry to our children was more important than our ministry in the local church. Their dad would reschedule or go late to meetings in order to attend all of their activities. We still change our schedule on occasions when we are the only ones who can meet their needs.

When we asked our children about the shift to friendship, they responded, "Our parents made an easy transition from parent to friend because the change wasn't drastic. It never happened; it just always was. They have somehow always been our parents and our friends. We don't believe that there will ever be a complete transition from parent to friend. They will always be both."

Families were intended to be religious societies,
in which the worship of God should be maintained, and in which means
should be used for training up children from generation to generation
in His fear and for His service.[1]

JOHN ANGELL JAMES

There have been times and places where John Angell James's opinion was the consensus view. Why did we drift so far away? It is because our natural bent is away from God, not toward Him. If our theology weakens, our obedience crumbles. One theologically careless generation begets a theologically ignorant generation. Result: rebellion. The following statements are characteristic of our time.

"I don't love him anymore. I dread waking up every day and living this lie of a Christian marriage. I have had it with his indifference and preoccupation with his job. I don't know how much longer I can stand this simmering separateness. Why should I live like this?"

"This marriage is a constant reminder of our child who died. I cannot look at my husband without thinking of our son. And yet it seems that he never thinks about our son because he will never talk to me about him. His impatience with my grief has built a wall between us. Surely God doesn't want me to live in this misery. Why shouldn't we just separate so we both can get on with our lives?"

"I knew in my head that Christians are not to be unequally yoked, but we were so in love that I didn't think it would make any difference. Now we live in two worlds. She says she wants the marriage to work, but I have grown spiritually, and I want a Christian wife. We don't have children, so why wouldn't it be best for us just to end it now?"

The situations are endless, but the question is basically the same. Isn't my personal happiness the primary goal in life?

The answer is yes, *unless* . . . unless there is a holy, majestic, transcendent, personal Glorious One who created us for a higher purpose.

The answer is yes, *unless* . . . unless there is a Glorious One who intimately entered time and place and redeemed us from sin for this higher purpose.

The answer is yes, *unless*. . .unless there is a Glorious One who enables His children to hear His Word with spiritual ears and empowers them to live above the pettiness of selfism and to fulfill the higher purpose—to be a reflection of His glory.

And there is.

CONNECTING THE DOTS

I am fascinated with the grand, overarching themes of Scripture such as redemption, covenant, presence, sovereignty, grace, and glory. These themes are not separate. They are strands of the same thread. They all point to the triune God. Scripture is God's revelation of Himself as the Creator, Redeemer, and Sustainer. Scripture declares His lordship over heaven and earth.

In the remaining chapters we will explore the theme of glory. The Hebrew word for glory, *kabod*, means heavy in weight. It has reference to the weighty importance, shining majesty, and brilliant light that accompany God's presence. It is that aspect of God that we as humans recognize and to which we respond in worship and obedience. When Moses asked to see God's glory, "the LORD said, 'I will cause all my goodness to pass in front of you.' . . . And he passed in front of Moses, proclaiming, 'The LORD, the LORD, the compassionate and gracious God, slow to anger, abounding in love and faithfulness, maintaining love to thousands, and forgiving wickedness, rebellion and sin'" (Exodus 33:19; 34:6-7).

We must understand the grand themes of Scripture in order to understand the individual parts of Scripture and the bits and pieces of our lives. If we don't connect the dots, represented by each fragment of life, to the overarching purpose of glorifying the Glorious

One, our thinking will be as clouded and distorted as the statements above. In the pressure of the moment, my happiness and security will become the overriding issue.

Just ask Peter.

BOLD INITIATIVES

When Peter saw Jesus walking on the water, he hopped out of the boat to meet Him (Matthew 14). This was a bold initiative, but it would have been foolhardy except for one glaring reality—Peter saw Jesus. As long as Peter gazed at the Glorious One, he walked above the circumstances of the moment. As soon as he glanced at the circumstances, he began to sink into them. The circumstances became the controlling factor in his life, and he would have drowned if he had not cried out to the Lord of those circumstances.

Glorifying God in our homes so that they become places of grace will require intentional initiatives that are as bold as Peter's exchange of the familiar for the faith-walk. One such initiative is to identify some core values for our families that will define who we are and how we live.

In each remaining chapter, we will consider instances when glory broke through in a time and place, and then we will identify a core value that flows from each glimpse of God's glory. Obviously, this list is just a starting point. You will doubtless want to identify other core values for yourself and your family.

God's glory must overshadow every relationship and situation. God shows us His glory in His Word. That is where we must fix our gaze, because what we believe about God will determine how we live. So let's begin with an overview of this theme in God's Word.

GLORY AT CREATION

Remember, the Hebrew word for glory, *kabod,* refers to the brilliant light of God's presence. Light was the first thing God commanded into existence: "Now the earth was formless and empty, darkness was over the surface of the deep, and the Spirit of God was hovering over the waters. And God said, 'Let there be light,' and there was light" (Genesis 1:2-3).

The power of God's Word broke through the darkness and hurled light into existence. In this initial creation act the brilliance of God's glory broke through the darkness, and creation itself could not remain silent. "The heavens declare the glory of God; the skies proclaim the work of his hands" (Psalm 19:1).

The light of God's glory shattered the darkness. It still does. "For God, who said, 'Let light shine out of darkness,' made his light shine in our hearts to give us the light of the knowledge of the glory of God in the face of Christ" (2 Corinthians 4:6).

The concept of light is very important in Scripture. Light symbolizes life and blessing. "For you have delivered me from death and my feet from stumbling, that I may walk before God in the light of life" (Psalm 56:13).

The Aaronic benediction is a prayer for God's blessing on His people. In this prayer, the desired blessing is not health and wealth. The ultimate blessing is for God to shine the light of His glory upon us.

> The LORD said to Moses, "Tell Aaron and his sons, 'This is how you are to bless the Israelites. Say to them: "The LORD bless you and keep you; the LORD make his face shine upon you and be gracious to you; the LORD turn his face toward you and give you peace."' So they will put my name on the Israelites, and I will bless them."
>
> NUMBERS 6:22-27

We will examine this prayer more in the next chapter, but for now let's continue to trace the theme of glory.

GLORY AT THE FALL

Adam and Eve sinned, and the darkness of evil entered the world. God could have left man in this miserable condition, but again glory penetrated the darkness. God dispelled the darkness by returning to the garden and revealing the light of His presence and His promise of salvation.

This promise that He would still be their God, and He would provide the way for them to live in His presence is unfolded throughout the Old Testament as we see manifestations of the shining brilliance of God's glorious presence with His people. The cloud and the pillar of fire led the Israelites through the wilderness. The splendor of Mt. Sinai accompanied the giving of the Law. When the tabernacle was completed, "the cloud covered the Tent of Meeting, and the glory of the LORD filled the tabernacle" (Exodus 40:34). This glory cloud is often referred to as the "shekinah" glory. This word is not used in the Bible. It is a transliteration of a Hebrew word that means "that which dwells." It is found in many Jewish writings that speak of God's presence and His nearness. Because of the covenant, God dwells among His people. We live in the light of His presence. The glory cloud over the tabernacle was a visible representation of this reality.

> *The LORD is my light and my salvation—whom shall I fear?*
> *The LORD is the stronghold of my life—of whom shall I be*
> *afraid?*
>
> PSALM 27:1

> *Blessed are those who have learned to acclaim you, who walk in*
> *the light of your presence, O LORD.*
>
> PSALM 89:15

GLORY AT THE INCARNATION

The world waited, and waited. Sometimes the silence seemed endless.

> *But when the time had fully come, God sent his Son, born of a*
> *woman, born under law, to redeem those under law, that we might*
> *receive the full rights of sons.*
>
> GALATIANS 4:4-5

Once again the light of God's glory shattered the darkness and brought life and blessing.

In the beginning was the Word, and the Word was with God, and the Word was God. He was with God in the beginning.
Through him all things were made; without him nothing was made that has been made. In him was life, and that life was the light of men. The light shines in the darkness, but the darkness has not understood it. . . .
The Word became flesh and made his dwelling among us. We have seen his glory, the glory of the One and Only, who came from the Father, full of grace and truth.

JOHN 1:1-5, 14

This is the message we have heard from him and declare to you: God is light; in him there is no darkness at all.

1 JOHN 1:5

The heavenly hosts could not remain silent. After the angel announced the news to the shepherds, "A great company of the heavenly host appeared with the angel, praising God and saying, 'Glory to God in the highest, and on earth peace to men on whom his favor rests'" (Luke 2: 13-14).

GLORY AT THE TRANSFIGURATION

One day Jesus took Peter, James, and John for a walk. To tell what happened that day, the gospel writers are at a loss for words. Matthew simply reports, "He was transfigured before them. His face shone like the sun, and his clothes became as white as the light" (Matthew 17:2). But what else could he say? Jesus' deity burst through, and human language could never describe that sight. This was not a reflected glory. This was "the brightness of His glory" (Hebrews 1:3 NKJV) that is intrinsic to Him as God.

The word *transfigure* is from the Greek *metamorphoo*, which means to change into another form. This revelation of Jesus' deity was a glimpse of the glory that all will see when He returns, and "at the name of Jesus every knee should bow, in heaven and on earth and under the earth, and every tongue confess that Jesus Christ is Lord, to the glory of God the Father" (Philippians 2:10-11).

GLORY AT THE CROSS

Creation groaned when our sins were laid upon the King of glory as He hung on the cross. "It was now about the sixth hour, and darkness came over the whole land until the ninth hour, for the sun stopped shining" (Luke 23:44-45).

Then when His redemptive work was accomplished and He gave up the ghost, "the curtain of the temple was torn in two" (Luke 23:45). This was the curtain that had blocked the entrance to the Holy of Holies. The ripping of the curtain shows that Jesus opened the way to the glorious presence of God: "We have confidence to enter the Most Holy Place by the blood of Jesus, by a new and living way opened for us through the curtain, that is, his body. . ." (Hebrews 10:19-20).

This right of entry carries personal privilege and responsibility: "And since we have a great priest over the house of God, let us draw near to God with a sincere heart in full assurance of faith, having our hearts sprinkled to cleanse us from a guilty conscience and having our bodies washed with pure water. Let us hold unswervingly to the hope we profess, for he who promised is faithful" (Hebrews 10:21-23).

This right of entry also carries corporate responsibility: "And let us consider how we may spur one another on toward love and good deeds. Let us not give up meeting together, as some are in the habit of doing, but let us encourage one another—and all the more as you see the Day approaching" (Hebrews 10:24-25).

GLORY AT THE TOMB

The body of Jesus was laid in a tomb, and a stone was rolled over the opening, but the darkness of the tomb was shattered by the bril-

liance of resurrection glory. The curse of death was broken by resurrection life.

> *He is before all things, and in him all things hold together. And
> he is the head of the body, the church; he is the beginning and the
> firstborn from among the dead, so that in everything he might have
> the supremacy. For God was pleased to have all his fullness dwell
> in him, and through him to reconcile to himself all things, whether
> things on earth or things in heaven, by making peace through his
> blood, shed on the cross. . . . God has chosen to make known
> among the Gentiles the glorious riches of this mystery, which is
> Christ in you, the hope of glory.*
>
> COLOSSIANS 1:17-20, 27

GLORY AT THE ASCENSION

Once again I am intrigued with the lack of words used to describe this
incredible event. It cannot be described. It is to be believed. This reality should shape our view of and relationship to this world and the
world to come.

> *After the Lord Jesus had spoken to them, he was taken up into
> heaven and he sat at the right hand of God. Then the disciples
> went out and preached everywhere, and the Lord worked with
> them and confirmed his word by the signs that accompanied it.*
>
> MARK 16:19-20

> *When he had led them out to the vicinity of Bethany, he lifted up
> his hands and blessed them. While he was blessing them, he left
> them and was taken up into heaven. Then they worshiped him
> and returned to Jerusalem with great joy.*
>
> LUKE 24:50-52

> *And after He had said these things, He was lifted up while they
> were looking on, and a cloud received Him out of their sight. And*

as they were gazing intently into the sky while He was departing,
behold, two men in white clothing stood beside them; and they also
said, "Men of Galilee, why do you stand looking into the sky? This
Jesus, who has been taken up from you into heaven, will come in
just the same way as you have watched Him go into heaven."

ACTS 1:9-11 NASB

This was the coronation of King Jesus. The conquering King returned to His homeland in a cloud. It was a cloud, the shekinah glory, that had covered the tabernacle and was the visible manifestation of God's presence among His people. This was a reminder of His covenant promise: "I will be your God, you will be my people, I will dwell among you."

King Jesus took His rightful place of honor and authority at the right hand of the Father. King David heralded this day when he said, "The LORD says to my Lord: 'Sit at my right hand until I make your enemies a footstool for your feet.' The LORD will extend your mighty scepter from Zion; you will rule in the midst of your enemies" (Psalm 110:1-2).

An article in *The New Geneva Study Bible* states:

The Ascension was from one standpoint the restoration of the glory that the Son had before the Incarnation, from another the glorifying of human nature in a way that had never happened before, and from a third the start of a reign that had not existed in this form before. . . . In sovereignty He now lavishes upon us the benefits that His suffering won for us. From His throne He sends the Holy Spirit constantly to enrich His people (John 16:7-14; Acts 2:33) and equip them for service (Eph. 4:8-12).[2]

Those who gazed at the departing Christ then went and preached everywhere, worshiped, and were filled with joy. This messy, motley group turned the world upside down. There was nothing spectacular about them, but they had gazed at the spectacle of glory, and they became a spectacle of grace.

The writer of Hebrews succinctly summarized the person and work of Jesus:

> *In the past God spoke to our forefathers through the prophets at many times and in various ways, but in these last days he has spoken to us by his Son, whom he appointed heir of all things, and through whom he made the universe. The Son is the radiance of God's glory and the exact representation of his being, sustaining all things by his powerful word. After he had provided purification for sins, he sat down at the right hand of the Majesty in heaven.*
>
> HEBREWS 1:1-3

Jesus is the Creator, Sustainer, Purifier/Redeemer. It is the person and work of this Glorious One that gives purpose and power to us and to our families.

GAZING AT GLORY

What does this mean for my family? What does it mean for people with questions like those at the beginning of this chapter? It means everything. Our knowledge of God's majestic glory is what will determine our response to every situation.

Peter gazed at the Glorious One and then activated his faith by stepping out of the boat. Our faith must be activated in every relationship and situation. Activating faith is not just an emotional response. Many times we must act on principle apart from emotion.

Gazing at glory is not a mystical, experiential exercise in otherworldliness. This is the hard stuff of studying truth and applying truth to everything we do.

This is the rubber-meets-the-road kind of substantive faith that says that God's Word is the rule for our family's faith and practice.

This is a growing knowledge of His goodness and a growing commitment to His glory.

And the wonder of it is that the doing of it is beyond my ability. It is all of grace.

Now in response to what we have seen about the Glorious One, let's identify a family value for those who live in the realm of the covenant. These family values will be countercultural because they do not exalt self; they glorify God. They reflect His goodness. These are the cultural values of the covenant community. They are expressions of the rubric of grace and the rule of love.

There will be a commonality of core values for families who live in the realm of the covenant, because these are biblical ethics, but there will be different emphases, priorities, and expressions of these values among families and in different life seasons. This diversity is good. It will make the work and worship of God's family richer and healthier.

Each core value is an expression of the boldest initiative ever decreed: "'Love the Lord your God with all your heart and with all your soul and with all your mind.' This is the first and greatest commandment. And the second is like it: 'Love your neighbor as yourself'" (Matthew 22:37-39).

A FAMILY VALUE—STEWARDSHIP

This principle governs life in the realm of the covenant. Everything we are and have is a gift from God. We are to be good stewards by using our life and gifts for His glory and not for selfish gain.

A life of stewardship is a lifestyle of worship. It is the daily offering of all that we have and all that we are "as living sacrifices, holy and pleasing to God—this is [our] spiritual act of worship" (Romans 12:1) because we understand that "He must become greater; I must become less" (John 3:30).

What will this look like? Here are a few examples.

•When a child exhibits an ability or develops a new skill, talk about this as a gift from the Lord and discuss how it is to be used for His glory. Whether the child has an athletic ability, can memorize Scripture easily, displays an interest in bugs, or learns to play a musical instrument, encourage him or her to be a good steward of that ability and opportunity.

• During the writing of this book, our family began a tradition. Gene and I took a Grand Trip. We took the two oldest grandchildren to the Grand Canyon, and we told the others that when they are older, we will take them, two at a time, on a special trip. We gave Hunter and Mary Kate notebooks with pages for journaling and for photos, and Bible study sheets. We studied passages on creation, and we memorized Revelation 4:11: "You are worthy, our Lord and God, to receive glory and honor and power, for you created all things, and by your will they were created and have their being." We were intentional in discussing our responsibility to be good stewards of God's creation and of the opportunity to visit that magnificent place. When we heard lectures from an evolutionary perspective, we talked about God's grace that had opened our hearts and minds to God's truth and our responsibility to be good stewards of that grace. All the while we were very aware that we must be good stewards of these children entrusted to our family.

• We are to be good stewards of our spouse's gifts and graces. We must be careful not to let our own insecurities or selfishness hinder our spouse from using his or her abilities for God's glory. Rather, we must celebrate and encourage the use of those gifts.

• We are to be a good steward of our season in life. The single person should offer his or her singleness to the Lord as an offering to be used for His glory. The young parents, the retired person, the elderly shut-in should all see each place on life's time-line as a sacrifice of praise to be given to the Lord.

• We are to be good stewards of our family's time, finances, gifts, and graces by using those resources to serve others. One mother told me that her teenage daughter has an intense passion for international students at her school. This daughter repeatedly suggested that they invite some of these students to their home for holidays, but this was not the mother's ministry interest, so she never picked up on the suggestion. Then it occurred to this mother that her child could be spiritually gifted in an entirely different way from herself. Yet, being a child, she would need her mother's support and encouragement in facilitating the use of those gifts. The mother concluded by saying, "I can happily report that we are now booked solid for Thanksgiving and Christmas with my daughter's friends."

•When Annie Grace died, I prayed that we would be good stewards of our grief and that we would discover the treasures of darkness: "I will give you the treasures of darkness, riches stored in secret places, so that you may know that I am the LORD, the God of Israel, who summons you by name" (Isaiah 45:3). One entry in my prayer journal said:

> Help us to suffer covenantally by staying in the Word and staying in the community. "You will keep him in perfect peace, whose mind is stayed on You, because he trusts in You" (Isaiah 26:3 NKJV). Help us to use our energy to think Your thoughts. Help us not to detach from the covenant community. If we withdraw into ourselves, they cannot weep *with* us as they are commanded to do (Romans 12:15). We will force them to only weep *for* us.

•We are to be good stewards of the marriage God has given us. Do we view our spouse and our lives together as a gift from God? When we return this gift to Him, will it have multiplied in value because we cared for it well?

•We can be good stewards of our home by offering "hospitality to one another without grumbling" (1 Peter 4:9).

•We are to exercise stewardship of the times of plenty and want, sickness and health, joy and sorrow. Do we see them with faith-eyes and learn the faith-lessons? Do we then share the gifts and graces of those lessons with the covenant family?

What does it look like? It looks like Jesus.

> *The Son of Man did not come to be served, but to serve, and to give his life as a ransom for many.*
>
> MATTHEW 20:28

This is a bold initiative.

Why should we live this way? Because we belong to the Glorious One, and our overarching purpose is to reflect His glory.

How can we live this way? By living in the grace zone. "We want you to know about the grace that God has given the Macedonian churches. For I testify that they gave as much as they were able, and even beyond their ability . . . but they gave themselves first to the Lord and then to us in keeping with God's will" (2 Corinthians 8:1, 3, 5).

What will motivate us to embrace this family value? The knowledge of His transcendent glory and His intimate love for us will develop a reverence and gratitude that will compel us to a life of stewardship.

How do we teach our children to live this way? By living this way and by telling them over and over why we do what we do.

THE ANCIENT PATH

Here is the ancient path, the good way. Meditate on it and walk in it.

> *Give to the LORD, O families of the peoples,*
> *Give to the LORD glory and strength.*
> *Give to the LORD the glory due His name;*
> *Bring an offering, and come before Him.*
> *Oh, worship the LORD in the beauty of holiness!*
> 1 CHRONICLES 16:28-29 NKJV

In this song composed in honor of the return of the ark of God's covenant, the symbol of His presence, to Jerusalem, David called the people to give the Lord the glory due His name.

Dr. Edward Payson, a beloved New England pastor, died in 1827, but his sermons live on in *The Complete Works of Edward Payson*. Be pastored by him as you read portions of his sermon on this passage:

> He who rightly performs this duty [to give to the Lord the glory due His name] will perform . . . every other duty which God requires of his creatures; for the whole preceptive part of the Bible is contained in this one command. . . .

If no praises are thought too great for the patriot, who
delivers his country from temporal bondage, what praises
are sufficient for him who offers to a ruined and enslaved
world, deliverance from sin and misery, and death and hell?
O, never, never, can any creature, nor all creatures com-
bined, give God the whole glory which his works
deserve. . . . All they can do is to give him all that they have,
to acknowledge that he alone is worthy to be praised, that
all glory and honor are his due, and to combine all their
powers, and all their affections and exertions in forming one
refulgent unequalled crown, not to be placed on his head,
for it would be unworthy, but to be cast at his feet. When all
creatures shall unite in doing this, when they shall all fear,
and admire, and love, and serve, and obey, and thank, and
praise Jehovah with their whole heart, and soul, and mind,
and strength, then, and not till then, will they obey the command which calls upon them to give him the glory which is
due to his name. This is done in heaven. There every heart
is filled to overflowing with all holy affections; every tongue
is loud in his praise; every crown is cast at his feet; saints,
angels, and archangels are all prostrate before him. And thus
it ought to be on earth. Thus it would be, were not men
alienated from God by sin and blind to the glories of his
nature, his character, and his works. . . .

Compare the blessings which have descended from
heaven to earth with the returns which have ascended from
earth to heaven. . . . From a comparatively small number of
families and individuals scattered here and there, see a few
clouds of incense, a few imperfect offerings, praises and
thanksgivings slowly ascending to heaven. . . .

So far as the blessings you have received exceed the
returns which you have made; so far as each of you has failed
to glorify God to the utmost extent of his powers, so far you
are indebted to him . . . let all, without delay . . . proceed to
present their bodies and their souls as living sacrifices to
God, continually offering those praises, thanksgivings, and

spiritual services, which are acceptable through Jesus Christ. . . . Be jealous for the honor of the Lord your God, and with increasing diligence and fervor and constancy, give unto him the glory which is due to his name.[3]

QUESTIONS AND ANSWERS

Q. My thinking is still a bit fuzzy. How do we determine our family values?
A. Pray and ask the Lord to give you a unity of heart and purpose. Talk about your situation, opportunities, and passions. Then prayerfully determine one core value that will begin to define your family. Talk and pray together as a family about this value. Ask the Lord to show you specific ways to activate this value in your family life. Once this value has become ingrained in the language and actions of your family, add another core value.

BIBLE STUDY

1. Read Psalm 27 several times.
    • What does this psalm teach about God?
    • What does the light of God's presence do for the psalmist?
    • What application does this have for you and your family?

2. Meditate on Hebrews 1:1-3.
    • What do you learn about Jesus in this passage?
    • What difference does this make in how you view the world and your life?

3. Read the following passages on the principle of stewardship, and then write a statement of application for your life and the life of your family.
    Luke 12:35-48
    1 Corinthians 4:1-2
    1 Peter 4:10

4. Memorize the Aaronic blessing (Numbers 6:22-27). Make this a part of your family worship each day.

8

The Just One

TELL THE NEXT GENERATION

Name Withheld

Susan: *Many struggle with their relationships with their parents. What have you learned about accepting and relating to your parents that can help others?*

A daughter: *For years, I begged God to help me overcome a real problem with anger that brought shame on His name, hurt the ones I loved most, and which I routinely defended as just part of my personality. I asked Him to show me the root of my anger problem and discovered through prayer and journaling that it had to do with my relationship with my mom. I realized that I was breaking the fifth commandment when I gossiped about her and that in fact I hated her. A trusted friend agreed to pray regularly for healing in this relationship and that I would be able to receive the gifts of personal repentance and healing. The intentional part of this journey took almost two years.*

My mom's life was literally consumed with self-pity. It manifested itself in many unhealthy ways. She blamed her own unhappiness on anyone who didn't meet her needs, beginning with my father. She made a habit of dredging up offenses that were several years old and filling the minds of my sisters and me with those stories. Nothing could ever be her fault, and when life's inevitable bumps came along, she dealt with them by retreating into hypochondria. She spent greater and greater portions of her days in bed as my sisters and I grew up, and we were made to feel uncaring if we didn't show concern for her current "illness." Levels of sympathy shown toward her established the pecking order in our family. It was pretty complicated, looking back on things.

In answer to my searching prayers and the prayers of a trusted friend, God showed me the real root of my anger: It was my own self-will. My mom's problems weren't the issue at all. I was a forty-year-old child, stamping my foot and demanding that my needs be met, just the way my mom had. We just had different symptoms.

God didn't require me to deny the realities of my upbringing. I did need to obey Him by honoring my mom with loving words and deeds, however. This attitude would be based not on her deserving behavior, but on the love and sacrifice He modeled for me, an undeserving sinner, on the cross. There is a great freedom in knowing that this honoring is not based on my emotions but on His love. My relationship with my parents will probably never be like that of many who had Christ at the center of their childhood home, but it is well on the way to becoming the best it can be. Jesus changed my relationship with my parents the way He has always confronted my sin—through reminding me of His love and showing me what to do by setting a loving example.

Among the many figures used in Scripture to represent the blessedness of heaven, none is more instructive and pleasing than that of a family. Domestic connections are the first in nature, and if the duties resulting from them were rightly discharged, they would be productive of the noblest enjoyments. [1]

cceptance is a huge issue in family life. If we do not feel accepted, we will not feel that we belong. Home should be a place that represents the blessedness of heaven. Home should be a place where we feel that we belong. Heaven will be like that because Jesus longs for us to be there with Him. He said so, and He did everything necessary to make it so. "Father, I want those you have given me to be with me where I am, and to see my glory, the glory you have given me because you loved me before the creation of the world" (John 17:24).

Most of us struggle with accepting the people and circumstances in our lives and with feeling accepted by others. Our performance orientation is heard in statements such as:

• *If my spouse were more sensitive, or organized, or sociable, or spiritual, or whatever, our marriage would be better.* And the unaccepted spouse knows he/she does not quite measure up to the standard.

• *If I were smarter, prettier, more talented, or whatever, I would like myself better.* And family and friends grow weary trying to shore up the self-absorbed melancholic.

• *If I had not had such a difficult childhood, or if I had a better job, or whatever, I could be a better spouse or parent.* And the dissatisfaction gradually becomes debilitating despair.

• *If I do more for the Lord, He will love me more.* And the guilt-ridden, hyperactive child of God eventually loses joy and grows weary of well-doing.

This type of thinking displays a theological problem—a failure to understand the glorious doctrine of justification by faith alone. Martin Luther said that justification by faith alone is the article upon which the church stands or falls.

John Calvin said, "The doctrine of Justification is now to be fully discussed, and discussed under the conviction, that as it is the principal ground on which religion must be supported, so it requires greater care and attention. For unless you understand first of all what your position is before God, and what the judgment [is] which he passes upon you, you have no foundation on which your salvation can be laid or on which piety towards God can be reared."[2]

This doctrine is an essential building block in a haven of grace because our acceptance of ourselves, our circumstances, and others will be in proportion to our understanding of our acceptance before the judgment seat of God.

DAZZLED BY GLORY

The apostle Paul's dramatic conversion experience is well known. Paul, the persecutor of Christians, received permission to travel to Damascus to find any men or women who professed Christ. As he neared the city, "suddenly a light from heaven flashed around him. He fell to the ground and heard a voice say to him, 'Saul, Saul, why do you persecute me?' 'Who are you, Lord?' Saul asked. 'I am Jesus, whom you are persecuting,' he replied. 'Now get up and go into the city, and you will be told what you must do'" (Acts 9:3-6).

Consider an interesting contrast. This enemy of the cross was confronted with the glory of the risen Christ, and he became a servant of the Lord Jesus. However, the enemies of the Lord at the tomb saw a dazzling light, and they were paralyzed with fear. "There was a violent earthquake, for an angel of the Lord came down from heaven and, going to the tomb, rolled back the stone and sat on it. His appearance was like lightning, and his clothes were white as snow. The guards were so afraid of him that they shook and became like dead men" (Matthew 28:2-4).

Paul's radical obedience following his view of glory is well documented:

Five times I received from the Jews the forty lashes minus one. Three times I was beaten with rods, once I was stoned, three times I was shipwrecked, I spent a night and a day in the open sea, I have been constantly on the move. I have been in danger from rivers, in danger from bandits, in danger from my own country-men, in danger from Gentiles; in danger in the city, in danger in the country, in danger at sea; and in danger from false brothers. I have labored and toiled and have often gone without sleep; I have known hunger and thirst and have often gone without food; I have been cold and naked. Besides everything else, I face daily the pressure of my concern for all the churches.

2 CORINTHIANS 11:24-28

Why such a difference between Paul and the soldiers at the tomb? It was not because Paul was less an enemy of the cross than the soldiers. When we zoom in close, we discover the answer. Paul saw more than just a dazzling light. What he saw absolutely transformed him.

In addition to the account given in Acts 9, Paul shared his testimony both before a mob in Jerusalem (Acts 22) and before King Agrippa (Acts 26). Neither was a friendly audience. His life was at stake in both instances. The one who persecuted Christians was now willing to be persecuted. What caused this astounding reversal? We need all three accounts to get the full story.

To the mob in Jerusalem he said:

"About noon as I came near Damascus, suddenly a bright light from heaven flashed around me. I fell to the ground and heard a voice say to me, 'Saul! Saul! Why do you persecute me?' 'Who are you, Lord?' I asked. 'I am Jesus of Nazareth, whom you are persecuting,' he replied. My companions saw the light, but they did not understand the voice of him who was speaking to me. 'What shall I do, Lord?' I asked. 'Get up,' the Lord said, 'and go into

*Damascus. There you will be told all that you have been assigned
to do.'"*

ACTS 22:6-10

To king Agrippa he testified:

*"About noon, O king, as I was on the road, I saw a light from
heaven, brighter than the sun, blazing around me and my companions. We all fell to the ground, and I heard a voice saying to
me in Aramaic, 'Saul, Saul, why do you persecute me? It is hard
for you to kick against the goads.' Then I asked, 'Who are you,
Lord?' 'I am Jesus, whom you are persecuting,' the Lord replied.
'Now get up and stand on your feet. I have appeared to you to
appoint you as a servant and as a witness of what you have seen
of me and what I will show you. I will rescue you from your own
people and from the Gentiles. I am sending you to them to open
their eyes and turn them from darkness to light, and from the
power of Satan to God, so that they may receive forgiveness of sins
and a place among those who are sanctified by faith in me.' So
then, King Agrippa, I was not disobedient to the vision from
heaven."*

ACTS 26:13-19

James Montgomery Boice writes, "What a thunderbolt in Saul's
intellectual sky! Saul was so sure of himself. . . . He believed that the
Christians were wrong. Suddenly, in this remote place—as barren as
the area in which the Ethiopian was traveling, without a Christian
anywhere around—there was a light from heaven, God spoke, and
God was Jesus."[3]

Notice the elements of Paul's conversion that we see in these
accounts:

Paul was not looking for Jesus.

The light of God's glory broke through the darkness of Paul's sin.

Paul asked, "Who are you, Lord?"

The second person of the Trinity answered, "I am Jesus."

Paul asked, "What do you want me to do?"

But there is still another essential piece of this story.

"And since I could not see for the glory of that light, being led by the hand of those who were with me, I came into Damascus. Then a certain Ananias, a devout man according to the law, having a good testimony with all the Jews who dwelt there, came to me; and he stood and said to me, 'Brother Saul, receive your sight.' And at that same hour I looked up at him. Then he said, 'The God of our fathers has chosen you that you should know His will, and see the Just One, and hear the voice of His mouth. For you will be His witness to all men of what you have seen and heard.'"

ACTS 22:11-15 NKJV

There it is! Here we see the reason for the difference between this enemy of the cross and the men at the tomb. The God of covenant faithfulness chose Paul to know and to see the Just One.

Before we explore the significance of Paul's knowing the Just One, look again at the elements of Paul's conversion. To say that it was radical is an understatement, and yet every conversion is dramatic and radical. Of course there are unique elements in Paul's conversion, but the essential elements are the same. We are all enemies of the living God, but glory breaks through the darkness of our hearts, and "God, who said, 'Let light shine out of darkness,' made his light shine in our hearts to give us the light of the knowledge of the glory of God in the face of Christ" (2 Corinthians 4:6).

When we understand that Jesus is God, the Just One, we will bow in submission and ask, "What do you want me to do?" Anything less is questionable.

THE JUST ONE

Ananias said that Paul would be a witness of what he had seen and heard, and indeed he was. Paul fearlessly proclaimed the glorious doctrine of justification by faith alone:

This righteousness from God comes through faith in Jesus Christ to all who believe. There is no difference, for all have sinned and fall short of the glory of God, and are justified freely by his grace through the redemption that came by Christ Jesus. . . . For we maintain that a man is justified by faith apart from observing the law.

ROMANS 3:22-24, 28

He was delivered over to death for our sins and was raised to life for our justification. Therefore, since we have been justified through faith, we have peace with God through our Lord Jesus Christ, through whom we have gained access by faith into this grace in which we now stand. And we rejoice in the hope of the glory of God.

ROMANS 4:25—5:2

But when the kindness and love of God our Savior appeared, he saved us, not because of righteous things we had done, but because of his mercy. He saved us through the washing of rebirth and renewal by the Holy Spirit, whom he poured out on us generously through Jesus Christ our Savior, so that, having been justified by his grace, we might become heirs having the hope of eternal life.

TITUS 3:4-7

This is what the guards at the tomb did not understand. They were terrified, but they were not justified. If we do not understand the doctrine of justification, we will remain like dead people.

Before the judgment seat of God, we all stand condemned. We are sinners, and the verdict we deserve is death. But the wonder of grace is that the only one who does not deserve the death sentence, the Just One, stands in the heavenly court and says, "Charge the debt of My covenant people to My account *and* add My righteousness to their account." On the basis of this transfer, God declares us to be justified.

The Westminster Shorter Catechism says: "Justification is an act of God's free grace, wherein he pardoneth all our sins, and accepteth us as righteous in his sight only for the righteousness of Christ imputed to us, and received by faith alone."[4]

We can do nothing to earn this grace. We are bankrupt. This verdict does not change the fact that we are still sinners. It changes our status. We can now stand in the presence of the Holy Judge and not be consumed by His holiness. We are actually welcomed and accepted because of the righteousness of Jesus. Not only is our debt paid in full, but also we are adopted into God's family and become co-heirs of what rightfully belongs to God's only begotten Son. Our status before God will never change because Jesus will never change.

Original sin leaves us naked and ashamed before God. Our own efforts are worthless. "All of us have become like one who is unclean, and all our righteous acts are like filthy rags; we all shrivel up like a leaf, and like the wind our sins sweep us away" (Isaiah 64:6).

But Jesus, the Just One, accomplished the great exchange. "I delight greatly in the LORD; my soul rejoices in my God. For he has clothed me with garments of salvation and arrayed me in a robe of righteousness" (Isaiah 61:10).

This robe of righteousness is given freely to me, but it cost Jesus His very life. He earned this righteousness by living a perfectly sinless life and offering that life as the sacrifice for my sin.

When Thomas Manton preached Christopher Love's funeral sermon after Love was beheaded, on August 25, 1651, Manton said, "There are two deep pits wherein you may bury your sins, and you shall never hear of them any more: the ocean of divine mercy and the grave of Christ. It is uncomely to see a man in his nakedness; you should be wrapped in the winding-sheet of Christ's righteousness. There is no shroud like that. Come thus to the grave, and the grave shall have no power over you."[5]

When Paul saw Jesus as the Just One, he understood, and he obeyed the heavenly vision of glory because, as he later wrote, "I am not ashamed of the gospel of Christ, for it is the power of God to salvation for everyone who believes, for the Jew first and also for the Greek. For in it the righteousness of God is revealed from faith to faith; as it is written, 'The just shall live by faith'" (Romans 1:16-17 NKJV).

Paul was driven by the realization that Jesus, the Just One, loved him. "For Christ's love compels us, because we are convinced that one died for all, and therefore all died. And he died for all, that those who live should no longer live for themselves but for him who died for them and was raised again" (2 Corinthians 5:14-15).

When God looks at me, He sees Jesus. I continue to sin, but this does not cause Him to love me less, because He sees Jesus. If I do more "good stuff," God will not love me more, because He already loves me just as He loves Jesus. I don't have to earn His acceptance. I am accepted because of Jesus. Again be pastored by Edward Payson as he describes the wonder of salvation:

> There is more of God, more of His essential glory displayed in bringing one sinner to repentance, and forgiving his sins, than in all the wonders of creation. In this work, creatures may see, if I may so express it, the very heart of God. From this work, angels themselves have probably learned more of God's moral character than they have ever been able to learn before. They knew before that God was wise and powerful; for they had seen Him create a world. They knew that He was good; for He had made them perfectly holy and happy. They knew that He was just; for they had seen Him cast down their own rebellious brethren from heaven to hell for their sins. But until they saw Him give repentance and remission of sins through Christ, they did not know that He was merciful; they did not know that He could pardon a sinner. And O! what an hour was that in heaven when this great truth was first made known, when the first penitent was pardoned! Then a new song was put into the mouths of angels; and while, with unutterable emotions of wonder, love, and praise, they began to sing it, their voices swelled to a higher pitch, and they experienced joys unfelt before. O how did the joyful sounds, His mercy endureth forever, spread from choir to choir, echo through the high arches of heaven, and thrill through every enraptured angelic breast; and how did they cry, with one voice, "Glory to God in the highest, on earth peace, and good will to man!"[6]

When the light of God's glory blazed upon Paul, God sent Ananias to tell him, "The God of our fathers has chosen you that you should know His will, and see the Just One. . . ."

Paul was a Jew. When Ananias said, "The God of our fathers," all of the Old Testament promises would have flooded Paul's mind. He knew the covenant promise, and now he understood that Jesus was the promise. Paul received the covenant blessing. God made His face to shine upon Paul.

THE COVENANT BLESSING

The LORD said to Moses, "Tell Aaron and his sons,
'This is how you are to bless the Israelites. Say to them:
"The LORD bless you and keep you;
the LORD make his face shine upon you and be gracious to you;
the LORD turn his face toward you and give you peace."'
So they will put my name on the Israelites, and I will bless them."

NUMBERS 6:22-27

This blessing begins with an acknowledgment that God is the source of blessing. It is a prayer for His presence, grace, and keeping power. The Fall separated mankind from God, plunged him into darkness, and brought him under the curse of death. Man could do nothing to reverse this predicament. God alone has power to bestow the ultimate blessing of light and life, and He did this by way of the covenant of grace. The concept of God as the life-giver comes to ultimate expression in John 3:16: "For God so loved the world that he gave his one and only Son, that whoever believes in him shall not perish but have eternal life."

When God turns His face toward us, it is a sign of His acceptance of us. "Blessed be the God and Father of our Lord Jesus Christ, who has blessed us with every spiritual blessing in the heavenly places in Christ . . . to the praise of the glory of His grace, by which He has made us accepted in the Beloved" (Ephesians 1:3, 6 NKJV).

This acceptance, this declaration of our justification, brings peace with Him. The word translated "peace" is the Hebrew word *shalom*. This word occurs more than 250 times and is one of the most important theological words in the Old Testament. It means more than absence of strife or war. The word involves the ideas of completeness, wholeness, harmony, fulfillment, unimpaired relationships with others, and fulfillment in one's undertakings. This peace is the result of God's covenant of grace. "But now in Christ Jesus you who once were far away have been brought near through the blood of Christ. For he himself is our peace, who has made the two one and has destroyed the barrier, the dividing wall of hostility, by abolishing in his flesh the law with its commandments and regulations" (Ephesians 2:13-15).

Does this have practical application in the day-by-day routine of life? Absolutely. The one who lives in the light of God's face and is at peace with Him can then reflect that acceptance and peace to others. "'Though the mountains be shaken and the hills be removed, yet my unfailing love for you will not be shaken nor my covenant of peace be removed,' says the LORD, who has compassion on you. . . . All your sons will be taught by the LORD, and great will be your children's peace" (Isaiah 54:10, 13).

THE COVENANT WARNING

The covenant blessing is the light of God's face. The curse is for God to turn His face away from us. Notice the familial and corporate nature of this warning.

> Say to the Israelites: "Any Israelite or any alien living in Israel who gives any of his children to Molech must be put to death. The people of the community are to stone him. I will set my face against that man and I will cut him off from his people; for by giving his children to Molech, he has defiled my sanctuary and profaned my holy name. If the people of the community close their eyes when that man gives one of his children to Molech and they fail to put him to death, I will set my face against that man and his family

*and will cut off from their people both him and all who follow him
in prostituting themselves to Molech."*

LEVITICUS 20:2-5

I don't think this is a license to police each other. I think it is a
call to pray for each other. Families and churches must pray urgently
and fervently for the light of God's face to show us the gods of this
world and to make us fearless in snatching our children from them.
Consider again Edward Payson's words:

> And now, parents, let me beseech you to think seriously of
> this. You have imparted to your children your own corrupt
> nature. . . . And in consequence . . . they will perish forever,
> unless these evils be counteracted. But God has in mercy
> put into your hands means to counteract them. Make
> known to them his works and his will. Pour into their ears
> his praises. Let them see that you think of nothing, care for
> nothing, fear nothing, and love nothing as you do him. Let
> them see that you care, comparatively, very little what their
> situation is in this world, provided they receive a Christian's
> portion in the world to come. Do this, and add fervent per-
> severing prayer; and the corrupt nature which they have
> derived from you shall be changed by God's grace, a new
> heart and a right spirit shall be given them, and they shall be
> thus prepared to perform the same good office for their
> children, which you have performed for them.[7]

Now based on our knowledge of Jesus the Just One and His
acceptance of us, let's identify a family value for those who live in the
realm of the covenant.

A FAMILY VALUE—ACCEPTANCE

The biblical ethic of acceptance is not the same as the cultural idol of
tolerance. The idol of tolerance is divorced from truth. It does not
recognize the reality of sin. It may sound virtuous, but in the end it

is evil. "There is a way that seems right to a man, but in the end it leads to death" (Proverbs 14:12). The purpose of acceptance is God's glory; thus His Word defines acceptance. The purpose of tolerance is man's indulgence of self; thus tolerance is defined by his word. Biblical acceptance is based on our acceptance by Christ. It rests on the doctrine of justification.

We who are strong ought to bear with the failings of the weak and not to please ourselves. Each of us should please his neighbor for his good, to build him up. For even Christ did not please himself but, as it is written: "The insults of those who insult you have fallen on me." For everything that was written in the past was written to teach us, so that through endurance and the encouragement of the Scriptures we might have hope. May the God who gives endurance and encouragement give you a spirit of unity among yourselves as you follow Christ Jesus, so that with one heart and mouth you may glorify the God and Father of our Lord Jesus Christ. Accept one another, then, just as Christ accepted you, in order to bring praise to God.

ROMANS 15:1-7

What will this look like? Here are a few examples.

• When we accept ourselves and our circumstances because there is a deep knowledge of our acceptance by God and His sovereign plan for us, we are free from self-absorption. This freedom releases us to love, accept, and enjoy others.

• There is a security that comes with understanding justification that untangles us from the need to have others approve of our choices by making the same choices. It is demonstrated by families who can learn from and accept those who make different educational choices for their children. It is demonstrated when the super-structured and the go-with-the-flow families can enjoy, strengthen, and balance each other.

• Acceptance is seen in families that push beyond the similar and the familiar to forge friendships with families across racial and economic boundaries and with families with a child with disabilities. They do not view these friends as projects, but as people to love and enjoy.

• Understanding justification frees us from a performance mentality. When we know that we cannot measure up, but God loves us anyway, we will realize that we don't have to earn His love. The more we live in this reality, the less we will have to manipulate and scheme to get others to love us more. And our acceptance of others will not be conditioned on their living up to our expectations.

• We will be quick to recognize our sin and to repent, because we know that forgiveness is full and free. The more we know the enormity of God's love, the more we see our unworthiness, and this drives us to Him for grace.

• A heart understanding of justification will dissolve social, economic, racial, gender, and age barriers. We are free to encourage and build up others in the family and in the body of Christ. The strong can give support, and the weak can accept it. This cultivates true unity in the family and between families in the realm of the covenant.

• Our parenting and grandparenting will be free from attempts to elevate ourselves through the accomplishments of our children. Children who think they must establish their own righteousness through accepted behavior eventually become so weary that they give up or become masters of deceit.

• We are free from self-serving arrogance. Our consuming desire to praise and glorify the Just One will create an atmosphere of acceptance, appreciation, and affirmation rather than competition, confusion, and conflict. The "A" atmosphere is a definitive mark of a place of grace, a place of peace and rest where even the one who has failed knows that sin will not be tolerated, but he or she will be accepted.

What does it look like? It looks like Jesus.

Come to me, all you who are weary and burdened, and I will give you rest.

MATTHEW 11:28

This is a bold initiative.

Why should we live this way? Because we belong to the Just One, and our overarching purpose is to reflect His glory.

How can we live this way? By living in the grace zone.

What will motivate us to embrace this family value? The knowledge of His declaration that we are justified in His sight because of the righteousness of the Just One will develop humility, reverence, and gratitude that will compel us to a life of acceptance.

How do we teach our children to live this way? By living this way and by telling them why we do what we do.

THE ANCIENT PATH

Here is the ancient path, the good way. Meditate on it and walk in it.

> *Now the Lord is the Spirit, and where the Spirit of the Lord is, there is freedom. And we, who with unveiled faces all reflect the Lord's glory, are being transformed into his likeness with ever-increasing glory, which comes from the Lord, who is the Spirit. Therefore, since through God's mercy we have this ministry, we do not lose heart.*
>
> 2 CORINTHIANS 3:17—4:1

We cannot fake acceptance. It is a gift of living in the freedom of God's acceptance that we give to others. It is a gift that we do not stop giving because it is a gift we do not stop receiving.

QUESTIONS AND ANSWERS

Q. My husband works a lot of overtime so that I can stay home with our children. What are some things I can do to uphold him as head of the household even though he is away so much? I'm afraid our children will suffer because he is not more available.

A. The answer begins with the mother's heart attitude about her husband's headship and his work. Your children will duplicate your attitude, whether it is accepting and appreciative or fearful and resentful. Begin by asking the Lord to search your heart and to take away any fear or resentment. Ask Him to give you grace to "be content with what you have, because God has said, 'Never will I leave you; never will I forsake you'" (Hebrews 13:5). It is helpful if husbands and wives have good discussions about domestic responsibilities so that the expectations of one match the willingness of the other. Then here are some things you can do with and for your family:

• Pray with your children for your husband all during the day. If you are on an outing, stop and thank the Lord that Daddy works so hard so that you can do these things.

• Talk about how thankful you are for a daddy who goes to work and provides for the family.

• Talk about him as the head of your family and pray that God will give him wisdom as he leads your family.

• Talk about the virtue of being a hard worker like Daddy.

• When he comes home, make it a big deal. Don't dump all the problems or the children on him as soon as he walks in.

• As a couple, discuss his reentry from work/traffic to home. How much time does he need before he can transition to involvement with family? What can you and the children do to facilitate this?

• When children must be disciplined, involve your husband even though he is not there, by saying things such as: "God says you are to obey, and your dad and I must obey the Lord and teach you His way."

• As children get older, and the issues get bigger, it is appropriate to say, "Your dad and I will pray about it and discuss it as soon as we can."

• Be sure that the children hear you affirm your husband and thank him for making it possible for you to be at home with the children.

The mother's attitude will carry the day. A friend told us that when his children were young, he was frequently away from home. His wife never complained, and she always maintained an awareness of him by talking to the children about their daddy and praying for him. Their children are now grown, and he once asked them how they felt about his absences when they were younger. To his surprise, they were not aware that he had been away so much. His assessment: "My kids think I am the greatest dad in the world because the greatest wife in the world has told them so."

BIBLE STUDY

1. Read the following passages several times. Make a list of some of the common themes. Write a summary statement of what each passage means to you.
   John 14:27
   John 16:33
   Romans 5:1-11
   Ephesians 2:14-22
   Colossians 1:19-22
   Philippians 4:6-7

2. Read 2 Corinthians 5:14-21. What does this teach us about accepting ourselves, our circumstances, and others?

The Sovereign Holy One

TELL THE NEXT GENERATION

George and Karen Grant, Franklin, Tennessee

Susan: *George and Karen, I have had the privilege of watching you make an incredible investment in the rising generation. You have laid aside your own plans in order to teach teenagers. Why are you so committed to the next generation?*

George and Karen: *Because we've just about given up on this one.*

We always seem to learn things the hard way. We have a proclivity for majoring on the minors and minoring on the majors. We have a difficult time recognizing what is actually important, what is genuinely precious, or what ultimately matters in this poor fallen world. So though we would like to claim that our commitment to the next generation has arisen out of some profound virtue, some deep insight, or some well-defined strategy, we can't. We must confess that we have arrived at most of our covenantal and educational convictions by default—the kind of default that is attributable solely to the grace and mercy of God.

It was not too terribly long ago that we were untempered zealots. We wanted to right every wrong and undertake every righteous cause. We committed ourselves to stand against all manner of injustice. We were determined to champion beauty, goodness, and truth—the essential elements of Christian civilization—wherever they might be threatened. We plunged headlong into social activism, political involvement, and cultural renewal.

Unfortunately, we found that we were hardly prepared for such an undertaking. We were woefully ignorant of the very legacy we wished to defend.

Unlike so many of the great leaders we looked up to, we were so poorly edu-cated that we didn't even know what we didn't know. When we compared our grasp of the issues, of the historical precedents that underlay those issues, and of the theological principles that defined those issues with the knowledge of any of the great men and women of the past who laid the foundations of our freedom, we were appalled.

What made matters even worse was that as we looked around, we really did not see many others who were significantly better prepared for the difficult challenges our culture posed. With no little consternation, we began to ask, "Where are the Martin Luthers for our day? Where are the John Calvins? Where are the Patrick Henrys? Where are the Augustines, the Knoxes, or the Kuypers? Where are the heroes?"

We drew a blank. Hope grew dim.

It was only then that we began to comprehend that the most important thing we could do for the rest of our lives was not undertake one more campaign, fight one more fight, or launch one more project—as worthwhile as all those things might be. It slowly dawned on us that in order to reap the benefits of stal-wart leadership, a people must make substantive investments far in advance. Leadership must be prayed for, planned for, and prepared for—it doesn't just happen. We know, we know, that is hardly earth-shattering news. But we had finally come to the realization that in order to bring about reconciliation, restora-tion, and reformation in our culture, we would have to commit ourselves to the multigenerational agenda of covenantal faithfulness—just as it had always been, just as it always would be.

The Scriptures speak eloquently of our responsibilities to effectively train up the next generation of leaders. These responsibilities have been part of the con-fession of faith of God's people from the earliest days. Indeed they constitute a primary application of the first and great commandment (Deuteronomy 6:4-5; Matthew 22:37-38). They constitute a central element in what it means for those who are saved to keep covenant with God: "And these words which I com-mand you this day shall be upon your heart, and you shall teach them diligently unto your children" (Deuteronomy 6:6-7). Alas, we were not arrested by the glorious opportunities presented by the next generation until we had effectively given up on our own.

We still want to right every wrong and undertake every righteous cause. We still try to commit ourselves to stand against all manner of injustice. We remain determined to champion beauty, goodness, and truth—the essential elements of Christian civilization—wherever they might be threatened. But today we do so with a whole host of similarly motivated co-laborers as we teach young men and women the wonders of math and science, the delights of history and language, and the marvels of art and music—and all from the perspective and application of the Christian worldview as derived from God's revelation so that they might joyously walk in God's gracious covenant as faithful disciples of their sovereign Lord.

And as a result, our hope grows brighter with every passing day. A new generation of leaders is ready to step across the threshold of the twenty-first century. Just in the nick of time.

Not for himself, but others are the blessings of heaven bestowed upon man;
and whenever, instead of diffusing them around, he devotes them exclusively
to his own gratification . . . he is the grave of God's blessings. . . .
How different this, from the gently rising hill, clothed to its summit with fruits
and flowers, which attracts and receives the dews of heaven, and retaining
only sufficient to supply its numerous offspring, sends the remainder in
a thousand streams, to bless the vales which lie at its feet.[1]

EDWARD PAYSON

Isaiah is a bigger-than-life kind of man. The book that bears his name passionately and eloquently presents an extensive array of information covering an expansive amount of time. I tremble to think of dipping into this book and pulling out a few nuggets to present in a few pages, but I can't resist. I want to get a glimpse of what he saw, and I want the implications of that vision to permeate my life as it did his. I pray that this brief encounter with Isaiah will launch you on a journey into his book. But the book is not about him. Isaiah and his book point us to Jesus.

Isaiah was not "a grave of God's blessings." His encounter with God's glory was a trajectory that thrust him into a life of justice, mercy, and humility. Gaze into God's Word and ask Him to open your spiritual eyes that you might see what Isaiah saw.

DAZZLED BY GLORY

In the year that King Uzziah died, I saw the Lord seated on a throne, high and exalted, and the train of his robe filled the temple. Above him were seraphs, each with six wings: With two wings they covered their faces, with two they covered their feet, and with two they were flying. And they were calling to one another:

*"Holy, holy, holy is the LORD Almighty; the whole earth is full
of his glory." At the sound of their voices the doorposts and thresh-
olds shook and the temple was filled with smoke.*

ISAIAH 6:1-4

In this passage two names are used for God. Lord, which is the
Hebrew *Adonai,* means sovereign. LORD, which is the Hebrew
Yahweh, is His personal name of covenant faithfulness. Coupled with
Almighty, this name portrays Him as the divine warrior. The repeti-
tion "Holy, holy, holy" indicates His incomparable holiness.
According to John 12:37-41, Isaiah saw Jesus.

Isaiah's response comes as no surprise. The more we know God,
the more we know ourselves.

*"Woe to me!" I cried. "I am ruined! For I am a man of unclean
lips, and I live among a people of unclean lips, and my eyes have
seen the King, the LORD Almighty." Then one of the seraphs
flew to me with a live coal in his hand, which he had taken with
tongs from the altar. With it he touched my mouth and said, "See,
this has touched your lips; your guilt is taken away and your sin
atoned for."*

ISAIAH 6:5-7

God's response shows His mercy to the humble and repentant.
Taking a coal from the altar symbolizes purification.

When God asked the next question, Isaiah did not even ask
where or what. It did not matter. He had seen the Sovereign Holy
One and had been touched by His mercy. "Then I heard the voice of
the Lord saying, 'Whom shall I send? And who will go for us?' And
I said, 'Here am I. Send me!'" (v. 8).

One has to wonder whether Isaiah was prepared for what came
next. Probably not. Who would have expected this? "He said, 'Go and
tell this people: "Be ever hearing, but never understanding; be ever
seeing, but never perceiving." Make the heart of this people cal-
loused; make their ears dull and close their eyes. Otherwise they

might see with their eyes, hear with their ears, understand with their hearts, and turn and be healed'" (vv. 9-10).

The incongruity is mind-boggling. He saw the Sovereign Holy One, and yet he heard that this holy God's message would be rejected. But Isaiah did not flinch. His view of God caused him to ask only one question: "Then I said, 'For how long, O Lord?' And he answered: 'Until the cities lie ruined and without inhabitant, until the houses are left deserted and the fields ruined and ravaged, until the LORD has sent everyone far away and the land is utterly forsaken'" (vv. 11-12).

Then there is a glimmer of hope. There will be a remnant. There always will be, because God is the covenant-keeper. "But as the terebinth and oak leave stumps when they are cut down, so the holy seed will be the stump in the land" (v. 13). Middle Eastern terebinth and oak trees can produce new growth even when they appear to be damaged beyond hope.

ISAIAH'S FAMILY

The incongruity in Isaiah's situation is not unusual. Often we think that if we live faithful lives that reflect God's glory, people will love us and the message we proclaim. We think that if our family reflects God's grace in our neighborhood, other families will queue up at our door to ask the "reason for the hope that you have" (1 Peter 3:15). Actually it is hard to live countercultural lives, and rejection is not unusual.

Isaiah knew from the beginning that he and his message would be rejected. Yet he did not hesitate. Why? Because he had gazed at God's glory. He had seen the Sovereign Holy One seated on His throne. Isaiah's mission was not about success. It was about obedience.

Now it's one thing for Isaiah to say, "Here am I. Send me," but he took his family with him. They actually became part of his message. I like that. I look forward to meeting his wife in heaven.

When God sent Isaiah to the wicked King Ahaz with a message,

He told Isaiah: "'Go out, you and your son Shear-Jashub, to meet Ahaz at the end of the aqueduct of the Upper Pool, on the road to the Washerman's Field'" (Isaiah 7:3).

The name Shear-Jashub means "a remnant will return." This child's name is a statement of Isaiah's faith in God's covenant promise. In his commentary on Isaiah, Derek Thomas explains:

> This is crucial to the whole of Isaiah's message. Ahaz was a covenant-breaker; he, and the people who followed him, would be forsaken. But within the elect nation there was another election: an election of grace. The remnant, a faithful company who survived even in the darkest of days, survived to fulfill God's covenant promise to save a people for himself (see 6:13). It is more than a little interesting that the promise given to Abraham, which included a word about his children, should also be symbolically recalled here also by Isaiah's son standing at his side while he delivered the Word of God![2]

The name of Isaiah's second child was also part of his message: "Then I went to the prophetess, and she conceived and gave birth to a son. And the LORD said to me, 'Name him Maher-shalal-hash-baz. Before the boy knows how to say "My father" or "My mother," the wealth of Damascus and the plunder of Samaria will be carried off by the king of Assyria'" (Isaiah 8:3-4).

Isaiah's wife may have been a prophetess, or this could be translated "the wife of a prophet." We do not even know her name, but we know her heart. She shared her husband's mission. I find it quite commendable that she would agree to give her infant son such a preposterous name!

This child's name meant "speed the spoil, hasten the booty." The *New Geneva Study Bible* explains, "The name signifies the rapid devastation of Syria, Israel, and Judah, but also the presence of God with the remnant and the impending fulfillment of God's word."[3]

I am greatly encouraged by the participation of Isaiah's family in his ministry. Isaiah knew in advance the hardships of his mission. His family would not be voted most popular. It would have been understandable if he had shielded them from the danger and disdain. But Isaiah had seen the Holy Sovereign One. He was not afraid to involve his family. This was an outward-focused family who faced a hostile world with a message of judgment and of hope.

Our families are called to do the same.

ISAIAH'S MESSAGE

Despite the intimidating expansiveness of Isaiah's message, we will plunge in and consider a piece of it that I think has particular applicability to family life in the realm of the covenant.

After announcing God's judgment on Israel and their impending exile in Babylon, Isaiah speaks of their redemption and return. He is a master wordsmith. These are glorious descriptions of God's kingdom. Isaiah 54 and 55 are a renewal of the covenant. Our hearts soar as we read words such as:

> *"Sing, O barren woman, you who never bore a child; burst into song, shout for joy, you who were never in labor; because more are the children of the desolate woman than of her who has a husband," says the LORD.*
>
> *"Enlarge the place of your tent, stretch your tent curtains wide, do not hold back; lengthen your cords, strengthen your stakes. For you will spread out to the right and to the left; your descendants will dispossess nations and settle in their desolate cities. Do not be afraid; you will not suffer shame. Do not fear disgrace; you will not be humiliated. You will forget the shame of your youth and remember no more the reproach of your widowhood. For your Maker is your husband—the LORD Almighty is his name—the Holy One of Israel is your Redeemer; he is called the God of all the earth. . . .*
>
> *"All your sons will be taught by the LORD, and great will be your children's peace. In righteousness you will be established: Tyranny will be far from you; you will have nothing to fear. Terror will be far removed; it will not come near you."*
>
> ISAIAH 54:1-5, 13-14

> *"Come, all you who are thirsty, come to the waters; and you who*
> *have no money, come, buy and eat! Come, buy wine and milk*
> *without money and without cost. . . . Surely you will summon*
> *nations you know not, and nations that do not know you will has-*
> *ten to you, because of the LORD your God, the Holy One of*
> *Israel, for he has endowed you with splendor."*
>
> ISAIAH 55:1, 5

This message of hope is also a call to repentance: "'Let the wicked forsake his way and the evil man his thoughts. Let him turn to the LORD, and he will have mercy on him, and to our God, for he will freely pardon. For my thoughts are not your thoughts, neither are your ways my ways,' declares the LORD" (Isaiah 55:7-8).

Covenant renewal begins with God's promise and demands our repentance. Repentance is an essential element of the gospel of grace. Jesus made this quite clear: "But unless you repent, you too will all perish" (Luke 13:5).

Then in chapter 56 Isaiah begins to show what a life of repentance will look like. It begins with worship and spills out into justice, mercy, and humility. John Calvin said: "The prophet shows what God demands from us. . . . He demands from us such a conversion as shall change our minds and hearts, that they may forsake the world and rise towards heaven; and next he likewise calls for the fruits of repentance."[4]

Woven through this section of Isaiah's message is a contrast between true and false worship. John Frame makes the following observations about worship:

> Worship is the work of acknowledging the greatness of our covenant Lord.
> . . . worship is homage, adoration. It is not primarily for ourselves, but for the one we seek to honor. We worship for His pleasure foremost and find our greatest pleasure in pleasing Him. Worship must therefore always be God-centered and Christ-centered. It must be focused on the covenant Lord. . . .

Throughout the whole Bible story—from eternity past until the new heavens and the new earth—God "seeks" worshipers (John 4:23). . . . in the Bible we read of God's going to enormous trouble over many centuries, culminating in the sacrifice of His own Son, to redeem a people to worship Him.

Redemption is the means; worship is the goal. In one sense, worship is the whole point of everything. It is the purpose of history, the goal of the whole Christian story. Worship is not one segment of the Christian life among others. Worship is the entire Christian life seen as a priestly offering to God. And when we meet together as a church, our time of worship is not merely a preliminary to something else; rather, it is the whole point of our existence as the body of Christ.[5]

Isaiah gives a practical corollary of the sacred privilege and responsibility of worship. In his day people were going through the motions of worship, but there was no heart for it. Apathy toward worship is a chronic problem among God's people. This dullness often numbs us into viewing worship as an event that we attend in order to evaluate its effectiveness. Isaiah's contrast of true and false worship jolts us to the reality that worship is a lifestyle that culminates in gathering with the covenant community each Sabbath to celebrate our relationship with God. Presenting ourselves as "living sacrifices, holy and pleasing to God" is our "act of worship" (Romans 12:1). We will consider three of the characteristics of true worship that Isaiah identifies.

TRUE WORSHIP CHARACTERIZED BY SABBATH-KEEPING

This is what the LORD says: "Maintain justice and do what is right, for my salvation is close at hand and my righteousness will soon be revealed. Blessed is the man who does this, the man who holds it fast, who keeps the Sabbath without desecrating it, and keeps his hand from doing any evil."

ISAIAH 56:1-2

"If you keep your feet from breaking the Sabbath and from doing as you please on my holy day, if you call the Sabbath a delight and the LORD's holy day honorable, and if you honor it by not going your own way and not doing as you please or speaking idle words, then you will find your joy in the LORD, and I will cause you to ride on the heights of the land and to feast on the inheritance of your father Jacob." The mouth of the LORD has spoken.

ISAIAH 58:13-14

There is no ambiguity here. I do not feel the need to comment— only the need to repent.

TRUE WORSHIP CHARACTERIZED BY HUMILITY

For this is what the high and lofty One says—he who lives forever, whose name is holy: "I live in a high and holy place, but also with him who is contrite and lowly in spirit, to revive the spirit of the lowly and to revive the heart of the contrite."

ISAIAH 57:15

The Sovereign Holy One who lives in the high and holy place does not live with the high and mighty. He lives with the humble. Once again I'm nailed. But Isaiah does not let up. Now he really exposes my selfism and pride.

TRUE WORSHIP CHARACTERIZED BY A LIFE OF JUSTICE AND MERCY

Is not this the kind of fasting I have chosen: to loose the chains of injustice and untie the cords of the yoke, to set the oppressed free and break every yoke? Is it not to share your food with the hungry and to provide the poor wanderer with shelter—when you see the naked, to clothe him, and not to turn away from your own flesh and blood?

ISAIAH 58:6-7

Then. . . In Isaiah's narrative this word pulsates with anticipation. It lifts us to a high place to see the results of true worship.

> *Then your light will break forth like the dawn, and your healing will quickly appear; then your righteousness will go before you, and the glory of the LORD will be your rear guard. Then you will call, and the LORD will answer; you will cry for help, and he will say: Here am I. If you do away with the yoke of oppression, with the pointing finger and malicious talk, and if you spend yourselves in behalf of the hungry and satisfy the needs of the oppressed, then your light will rise in the darkness, and your night will become like the noonday.*
>
> ISAIAH 58:8-10

The prophet Micah was a contemporary of Isaiah. He gave the condensed version of this message:

> *With what shall I come before the LORD and bow down before the exalted God? Shall I come before him with burnt offerings, with calves a year old? Will the LORD be pleased with thousands of rams, with ten thousand rivers of oil? Shall I offer my firstborn for my transgression, the fruit of my body for the sin of my soul? He has showed you, O man, what is good. And what does the LORD require of you? To act justly and to love mercy and to walk humbly with your God.*
>
> MICAH 6:6-8

In his book *The Micah Mandate: Balancing the Christian Life*, George Grant calls Micah 6:8 "a lodestone of authenticity . . . a benchmark of balance."[6] He says:

Biblical balance is a happy melding of devotion and action, being and doing, patience and passion. It manifests word and deed, faith and works, forgiveness and discipline. It is a careful integration of the inner life and the outer life. It makes quiet conviction the natural companion of strident confession. It enables the head to coincide with the heart. Without compromising God's grace, it reveres God's decrees. Without suppressing spiritual liberty, it upholds spiritual responsibility.

In other words, it is mature.

And in a day marked by its notable revolt against maturity, biblical balance is a rare commodity indeed. Extremes dominate. One-dimensional obsessions control our churches, our discussions, and our lives. A thousand competing programs, projects, or paradigms lay exclusive claim on our limited time, attention, and resources. A kind of spiritual balkanization process has thus blurred our sharpest focus and muffled our best efforts.

But it need not be so.

Biblical balance is more practical than pragmatism. It is more thoughtful than rationalism. It is more experienced than existentialism and more romantic than sentimentalism. It is more stable than conservatism and more progressive than liberalism.

A faithful return to that kind of balance could very well be the harbinger of hope, the clarion cry for revival, that we so desperately long for in these dire days.[7]

Biblical balance is a mark of a place of grace, and this kind of maturity begins by gazing at the Sovereign Holy One. Then we will cry with Isaiah: "'Woe to me!' . . . 'I am ruined! For I am a man of unclean lips, and I live among a people of unclean lips, and my eyes have seen the King, the LORD Almighty'" (Isaiah 6:5).

Worship and repentance are the wellspring of a life of justice, mercy, and humility. The family value that flows from this glimpse of glory is a no-brainer.

A FAMILY VALUE

Justice, mercy, and humility are as expansive as Isaiah's message. This is a lifestyle. A family that embraces this value will not just sign up to help at the local homeless shelter or make regular visits to the nursing home. The heart of this family will beat with a passion for justice and a love for mercy because they have bowed in humility before the Sovereign Holy One.

What will it look like? It will look as radical as Isaiah's family. In our neighborhoods our homes will be places of truth and hope. They will be places of welcoming hospitality and impartiality. Our families will demonstrate justice, mercy, and humility to the irritating neighbor, the single mom, the troublesome relative, and the lonely widow. Some will have occasion to show mercy in dark places—where no one will see or applaud and where the recipient scorns their mercy. And some families may even be called upon to look like Opal Hardgrove's family.

BEN AND OPAL

This story is about a family, a church, and the world. It is laced with justice, mercy, and humility.

Ben Hardgrove was twenty-eight when an accident left him with a severe brain injury. Ben and his wife, Opal, had only one child, who was four years old. When the doctors recommended that Ben be institutionalized because his injury left him unable to control his emotions, Opal refused. She cared for him and learned all she could about how to help him. Her steadfast and merciful commitment to Ben led to his improvement far beyond the prognosis given by his doctors. In 1998 JC Penney presented Opal with the Golden Rule Award for her work in helping to establish the Brain Injury Association of Georgia. Opal shares her testimony with us.

> Before Ben's accident I was a free spirit with a hard, cold, empty heart. I was selfish. As I sat in the intensive care waiting room, I was struck with the fragility of life. Shortly before the accident, Ben had decided that our family should be in church. The people of the church we had visited rallied around me. One of the older women encouraged me

to read Isaiah 55 to Ben. I didn't have a Bible. I never thought I needed one. This dear woman gave me a Bible, and I began reading that passage to Ben each day. Through that passage and the ministry of the people in that church, I came to know Christ as my Savior.

Through the years of rehabilitation with Ben, Christ taught me much of His love and care for His children. About twelve years after the accident, God opened the door for me to go on a short-term mission trip. I was hooked. God gave me a passion to touch the hurting and lost with the mercy that had reached out to me.

Soon I began working for Mission to the World, the mission agency of the Presbyterian Church in America, as a project administrator. I take groups on short-term mission trips. Before my first trip to Peru, I asked the Lord to break my heart with things that break His heart. And break my heart He did. I had never seen such poverty. I was broken when I saw the street boys ministry and heard the stories of how these boys survive. Because their families are unable to care for them, boys are turned out of the home, many as young as four years old. The main item of their diet is often soap and dirt because it gives them a sense of fullness.

I cannot imagine never knowing what it means to be loved and cared for and to be abandoned by the one person who should love you—your mother. I still have vivid memories of how God took me when I was still a sinner, hungering for what I did not know, and in His mercy brought me to Himself. His love compels me to reach out to these dear boys. His Word tells us that "Religion that God our Father accepts as pure and faultless is this: to look after orphans and widows in their distress and to keep oneself from being polluted by the world" (James 1:27).

Opal makes several trips a year to Peru and has an incredible ministry to the street boys. Occasionally Ben is able to accompany her.

Opal and Ben were not able to have more children, but many boys in Peru call her Mama Opal.

I asked Opal and Ben's daughter Hope what it was like growing up in their home. This is her response:

> Growing up with my unique family has had its share of challenges but also a unique set of joys. It has been amazing to watch my mother love my father as he is, but also to do everything she can to honor him as head of the home. She has been incredibly supportive of me and the things I have been involved in. She is simply full of love to the point that she can't hold it in. It is a natural extension of the love she has found in Christ to love my father, to love me, and to love children all over the world that she has had an opportunity to meet and care for. I only hope that I continue to grow in Christ and that He will bless me with just a few of the gifts He has given my mom.

A covenant community extended mercy to a young family even though they knew this was not a short-term commitment. A young wife experienced the saving grace of the Sovereign Holy One, and she was empowered to humbly accept her situation and to offer costly mercy. From this crucible of suffering, a life of justice, mercy, and humility emerged.

What does it look like? It looks like Jesus. "He got up from the meal, took off his outer clothing, and wrapped a towel around his waist. After that, he poured water into a basin and began to wash his disciples' feet, drying them with the towel that was wrapped around him" (John 13:4-5).

This is a bold initiative.

Why should we live this way? Because we belong to the Sovereign Holy One, and our overarching purpose is to reflect His glory.

How can we live this way? By living in the grace zone.

What will motivate us to embrace this family value? The knowledge of His sovereignty and holiness and the grace of His purifying mercy will develop in our lives a reverence, humility, and gratitude that will compel us to practice justice and mercy.

How do we teach our children to live this way? By living this way and by telling them over and over why we do what we do.

THE ANCIENT PATH

Here is the ancient path, the good way. Meditate on it and walk in it.

> *The Spirit of the Sovereign LORD is on me, because the LORD has anointed me to preach good news to the poor. He has sent me to bind up the brokenhearted, to proclaim freedom for the captives and release from darkness for the prisoners, to proclaim the year of the LORD's favor and the day of vengeance of our God, to comfort all who mourn, and provide for those who grieve in Zion— to bestow on them a crown of beauty instead of ashes, the oil of gladness instead of mourning, and a garment of praise instead of a spirit of despair. They will be called oaks of righteousness, a planting of the LORD for the display of his splendor. . . . Their descendants will be known among the nations and their offspring among the peoples. All who see them will acknowledge that they are a people the LORD has blessed.*
>
> ISAIAH 61:1-3, 9

May our families embrace this mission and leave this legacy.

QUESTIONS AND ANSWERS

Q. How do we balance jobs, school, church responsibilities, and quality family time so that there is time for deeds of justice and mercy?

A. Perhaps the problem is that we think about these as separate entities and then try to equalize time for each. We need to consciously remember that the various parts of our lives are integrated around the singular purpose of glorifying God. This will require deciding what is most important and then regulating our family life accordingly. Admittedly this is easier if you start out with this focus, but it can be done regardless of the age and activities of your children. We will not be able to do everything all the time. We need to look at life in chunks and not in minutes or even days. And we need to remember that children learn as much, perhaps more, from our attitudes as from our actions.

Rather than teaching children to resent Dad's job, teach them to see his job as the family's ministry. Pray for him to have wisdom to glorify God in his work and to show God's love and mercy to his coworkers.

Meal times are prime opportunities to discuss current events. Once a week have everyone sign a card to send to a Christian who is standing for truth in the public square, or to a missionary, or to the director of a homeless shelter.

It seems to me that we often have a faulty concept of quality family time. As I look back over our years of parenting, our highest quality times were when we worshiped and worked together. What can a family do that is of higher significance and benefit than to join in the corporate worship of the Lord God? Regular participation in church life taught our children their most valuable lessons and provided our richest family times. Taking meals to the sick and visiting the elderly were things we did together.

Family chores helped us learn important skills and habits. Our adult children—even our daughters—can mow a lawn or paint a room because they grew up helping do these things. And with our projects there was only one way to do them—RIGHT! Gene still insists that if it's worth doing, it's worth doing well. Working together also taught our children "stick-to-it-ive-ness." Any task worth doing is worth completing. Every task is to be done for God's glory. The kids often grumbled, but now I smile when I hear them telling their kids the same thing.

BIBLE STUDY

1. Read Isaiah 6 and pray that you will have a greater understanding of God's sovereignty and holiness.

2. Read Isaiah 55, the chapter Opal was encouraged to read to Ben.

3. Read Isaiah 58.
   • Make a list of the things God tells us to do in verses 6-7.
   • What are the results in verses 8-9?
   • Make two columns: "If" and "then." List the "ifs" and "thens" that are given in verses 9b-14.

4. Read Isaiah 60.

10

The Risen, Reigning One

TELL THE NEXT GENERATION

Name Withheld

Susan: *Dear friend, I have watched you and your children display huge measures of grace as you have gone through the trial of being abandoned by your husband/father. Please tell us what you have learned.*

A Single Mother: *Of all the possible circumstances of life, one I never envisioned for myself was being a single mom. I married a man who I believed loved God and me. I had great confidence to bear four children because my husband was always so helpful and delighted in each child. But at forty-five, I found myself divorced and abandoned to rear children ages nine, eleven, sixteen, and eighteen alone.*

Early on it was clear to me that we needed the body of Christ. My children had always been taught that the church was family, so when all of their grandparents died and their father left, the church was the only place where all the puzzle pieces of life still seemed to fit. Many of our elders spoke with each child individually. Deacons asked often about my financial situation and let me know of their willingness to help wherever needed. Most of our friends made sure there was no change in their relationship with us and did not make an issue of the obvious change in our family. But if we wanted to talk, they listened. Not once did I feel condemnation from the body of Christ. With godly church leadership, families who remained close, and our resolve to find God's strength and joy in the situation, my children and I began to witness His faithfulness in new ways every day.

The greatest joy I found was in seeing that my children had been indoctri-

nated into a proper view of God. They kept believing Him when their prayers were not answered as they desired. I struggled with "keeping the faith" many times, only to have one of them remind me that our Lord remained faithful, even in the dark.

One evening I wept bitterly and cried out, "What are we going to do?" My daughter put her arms around me and replied, "We are going to do what we have always done—trust God." They have helped me rejoice over the daily provision from His hand and have given thanks for the obvious protection that we used to take for granted. They frequently remind me that all things work together for good for His chosen people. This proper understanding of God has inhibited the bitterness that takes hold in most divorces. Bitterness then prevents forgiveness. And in divorce there is need to forgive every day, just as Christ also forgives us. As we do not yet know the "end of the story," the children and I are often led by the Spirit to pray for their father.

We are still a covenant family. There is a sadness that will never leave us, but there is an even greater joy in what we have learned. Our God is "a father to the fatherless, a defender of widows. . . . God sets the lonely in families . . . but the rebellious live in a sun-scorched land" (Psalm 68:5-6). I used to believe that the home of a single mom could only be a "sun-scorched land." Now I know that is not true. His presence can make any family rich. I have a beautiful life because His grace is sufficient.

Parents, as you would wish your instructions and admonitions
to your family to be successful, enforce them by the power of a holy example.
It is not enough for you to be pious on the whole, but you should be
wholly pious. . . . To some parents I would give this advice, "Say less about
religion to your children, or else manifest more of its influence. Leave off
family prayer, or else leave off family sins."[1]

J O H N   A N G E L L   J A M E S

e're back to Stephen, the one who started my journey, gazing at glory as I grieved the death of our granddaughter Annie Grace. Stephen brings us face to face with the great reality of life: Jesus Christ is the Risen, Reigning Lord of Glory.

Nine months after Annie was transferred to the church triumphant, the day before her first birthday, I revisited Stephen. This time I was drawn to two other encounters with glory that we see in Scripture. At first these may seem to be unrelated events, but that day the connection comforted and challenged me. I saw with clearer eyes that what we know about God will determine how we and our families live. I pray that you will be comforted and challenged, as I was, by the following recurring themes in these episodes:

Fiery trials will come to God's covenant people.

God keeps His covenant promise—"I will be your God; I will be with you."

God's presence empowers us in times of adversity and suffering.

Obedience in the trials opens our spiritual eyes to see more of God's glory.

We must *know* the character and promises of God in order to *act* upon them in times of crisis.

SHADRACH AND COMPANY

The story is well known. King Nebuchadnezzar built an image of gold and said everyone must bow down to it or be thrown into the fiery furnace. Shadrach, Meshach, and Abednego refused. When Nebuchadnezzar gave them one more chance to bow to his image, he asked the question that the enemy of our souls whispers to us whenever trials come: "What god will be able to rescue you from my hand?" (Daniel 3:15).

Shadrach, Meshach and Abednego replied to the king, "O Nebuchadnezzar, we do not need to defend ourselves before you in this matter. If we are thrown into the blazing furnace, the God we serve is able to save us from it, and he will rescue us from your hand, O king. But even if he does not, we want you to know, O king, that we will not serve your gods or worship the image of gold you have set up."

DANIEL 3:16-18

We need to be ready with this answer whenever we are challenged to fear or doubt. God is able; we are yielded. Trust and obey. We also need to know that the crisis may not go away. It may get worse.

Then Nebuchadnezzar was furious with Shadrach, Meshach and Abednego, and his attitude toward them changed. He ordered the furnace heated seven times hotter than usual and commanded some of the strongest soldiers in his army to tie up Shadrach, Meshach and Abednego and throw them into the blazing furnace.

DANIEL 3:19-20

The fire was so hot that the soldiers who threw them in were killed. The Biblical narrative is riveting:

Then King Nebuchadnezzar leaped to his feet in amazement and asked his advisers, "Weren't there three men that we tied up and threw into the fire?" They replied, "Certainly, O king."

He said, "Look! I see four men walking around in the fire, unbound and unharmed, and the fourth looks like a son of the gods."

Nebuchadnezzar then approached the opening of the blazing furnace and shouted, " Shadrach, Meshach and Abednego, servants of the Most High God, come out! Come here!" So Shadrach, Meshach and Abednego came out of the fire, and the satraps, prefects, governors and royal advisers crowded around them. They saw that the fire had not harmed their bodies, nor was a hair of their heads singed; their robes were not scorched, and there was no smell of fire on them.

Then Nebuchadnezzar said, "Praise be to the God of Shadrach, Meshach and Abednego, who has sent his angel and rescued his servants! They trusted in him and defied the king's command and were willing to give up their lives rather than serve or worship any god except their own God."

DANIEL 3:24-28

There have been countless debates over whether the fourth person in the fire was a preincarnate appearance of Jesus or an angel. Scripture does not tell us, but what is clear is that God kept His covenant promise: "I will be your God; I will be with you." Because God kept that promise, these men came out of the fire purer and stronger rather than scorched and smelly.

Dr. Sinclair Ferguson points out two characteristics of their faith:

(1) They had confidence in the power of God. . . . Yet as with all true faith, their confidence was not blind to the realities of the situation nor to the fact that God works out His purposes in the way He chooses, not in the way we would choose. So there was a second element to their faith.

(2) They were completely submissive to God's will, whatever that might be. . . . In the last analysis, the friends' faith was not in their deliverance but in their God. It was of the same order as Job's: "Though He slay me, yet will I trust Him" (Job 13:15). With Paul, they wanted to glorify God in their body either by life or by death. In a sense it was all one to them, as

long as God's name could be exalted (cf. Phil. 1:20). . . . Notice
that these men of faith would not have regarded their deaths
in the flames to be a failure of faith but rather an indication of
God's will. . . . Faith means trusting in God and His word.
Faith does not mean that we either know or understand what
His specific purpose in our lives may be. It means a ready willingness to follow Him whatever His purpose.[2]

Because of the fire, Shadrach, Meshach, and Abednego experienced an incredible intimacy with the reigning Lord of glory, who
kept His covenant promise to be with His children. I suspect they
were hesitant to leave the fire.

A STORM

In Matthew 14 we read that Jesus saw a crowd of people following
Him, and He "had compassion on them and healed their sick" (v. 14).
Jesus then cared for the people's need by feeding them—5,000 men
plus the women and children. Then the disciples got into a boat and
headed for the other side of the Sea of Galilee. Early the next morning, the waters became so turbulent that their boat was tossed from
wave to wave. Their terror was intensified when they saw something,
or Someone, walking on the water. Peter realized it was Jesus and
embarked on his famous trip atop the waves. There are so many mega-
events going on here that it is easy to miss a pertinent bit of information. Why were they in the middle of the sea?

"Jesus made the disciples get into the boat and go on ahead of
him to the other side . . ." (v. 22). The disciples did exactly what Jesus
told them to do; they were exactly where He told them to be, and a
storm came. Into their storm-tossed life Jesus came, and He spoke:
"Take courage! It is I. Don't be afraid" (v. 27).

Because of the storm the disciples saw a marvelous manifestation
of God's glory. They saw Jesus come to them in the midst of the
storm. He came at an unexpected time and in an unexpected way. But
He came. He always does.

STEPHEN

It began with some trumped-up charges against Stephen. The kingdom of darkness can never deal in truth. Stephen was brought before a shocked Sanhedrin, for as they looked at him "they saw that his face was like the face of an angel" (Acts 6:15).

Stephen began his defense by referring to the God of glory and the covenant promise:

> *"Brothers and fathers, listen to me! The God of glory appeared to our father Abraham. . . . God promised him that he and his descendants after him would possess the land, even though at that time Abraham had no child. . . . Then he gave Abraham the covenant of circumcision. And Abraham became the father of Isaac and circumcised him eight days after his birth. Later Isaac became the father of Jacob, and Jacob became the father of the twelve patriarchs."*
>
> ACTS 7:2, 5, 8

Stephen traced their history, which was a progressive revelation of the covenant of grace. Then he went for the jugular by pointing to their spiritual pride:

> *"You stiff-necked people, with uncircumcised hearts and ears! You are just like your fathers: You always resist the Holy Spirit! Was there ever a prophet your fathers did not persecute? They even killed those who predicted the coming of the Righteous One. And now you have betrayed and murdered him—you who have received the law that was put into effect through angels but have not obeyed it."*
>
> ACTS 7:51-53

Unregenerate hearts are always repelled by the gospel of grace:

> *When they heard this, they were furious and gnashed their teeth at him. But Stephen, full of the Holy Spirit, looked up to heaven and saw the glory of God, and Jesus standing at the right hand of*

*God. "Look," he said, "I see heaven open and the Son of Man
standing at the right hand of God."*

ACTS 7:54-56

Stephen saw the Risen, Reigning One standing. How extraordinary. In other places we read of Jesus sitting at the right hand of God (Colossians 3:1; Hebrews 10:12). Here Jesus stands to defend and to receive Stephen. The King of Glory stood to welcome His faithful servant. It was this sight of the Risen, Reigning One that overruled the horror and pain of the ensuing moments.

*At this they covered their ears and, yelling at the top of their voices,
they all rushed at him, dragged him out of the city and began to
stone him. Meanwhile, the witnesses laid their clothes at the feet
of a young man named Saul. While they were stoning him,
Stephen prayed, "Lord Jesus, receive my spirit." Then he fell on
his knees and cried out, "Lord, do not hold this sin against them."
When he had said this, he fell asleep.*

ACTS 7:57-60

Stephen saw glory, and he reflected glory by imitating Jesus. From the cross Jesus had uttered the same prayer for his tormenters: "Father, forgive them, for they do not know what they are doing" (Luke 23:34).

Because of the stones, Stephen saw the glory of the Risen, Reigning One. He saw the intimate love of the Savior who stood to welcome him.

LIFE LESSONS

There are several life lessons in these passages that I believe will help our families to stay on the forgotten paths that lead us to deeper intimacy with Jesus. These lessons will help protect us from the corrosive influence of selfism and materialism and will steady and strengthen our families.

•We can be in the way of obedience when the fires, storms, and stones come. We must resist the notion that trials necessarily mean that we have failed or that we have been disobedient.

•We must remember that God is always with us and He is in control. He can and will command the storm to cease in His time.

•If we gaze at glory, we can go through the fires, storms, and stones and actually come forth stronger.

•We can reflect God's glory in those times by forgiving those who are tormenting us.

•The fires, storms, and stones are God's mercy in our lives, because they allow us to see a greater manifestation of His glory and to experience a deeper intimacy with Him.

The overriding lesson is: God keeps His covenant promise.

> *But now, this is what the LORD says—he who created you, O Jacob, he who formed you, O Israel: "Fear not, for I have redeemed you; I have summoned you by name; you are mine. When you pass through the waters, I will be with you; and when you pass through the rivers, they will not sweep over you. When you walk through the fire, you will not be burned; the flames will not set you ablaze."*
>
> ISAIAH 43:1-2

I pray that you feel compelled to put this book down and worship the Risen, Reigning One who makes such a priceless promise to His covenant people.

Our view of God determines our view of everything and everyone else. This is the grand lesson of life that one generation is to commend to the next generation. This vibrant trust in God leads to worldview thinking and living. It will not be communicated just through formal teaching. It will be communicated by the way we live when we are in the fire and in the storm. It will be taught to the next generation by the way we respond to turbulent circumstances and to the people who throw stones.

I saw this vividly illustrated when we were on a family vacation.

I was sitting on the beach and saw son-in-law Dean walking down the path toward me. Even if I had not been able to see his face, I would have known that it was Dean because of the characteristic gait, the tilt of his head, and the swing of his right arm while the left hand was thrust into his pocket. Dean was oblivious to the uniqueness of his walk—he was just walking. But immediately behind him was nine-year-old Hunter. I laughed out loud as I took in my grandson's exact duplication of the gait, tilt of head, and even the swing of the right arm and the left hand in a pocket. Dean never gave Hunter a lesson in walking. Hunter never consciously set out to walk just like his dad. It just happened. So it is with most life lessons. So it is with core values that define a family.

FAMILY VALUE—FORGIVENESS

What core values flow from the glimpses of glory we have seen in this chapter? One of the obvious ones, and an essential one for a place of grace, is forgiveness. When God forgives, He binds us to Himself and to one another. John Calvin beautifully explained this phenomenon: "Forgiveness of sins, then, is for us the first entry into the church and Kingdom of God. Without it, there is for us no covenant or bond with God. . . . Not only does the Lord through forgiveness of sins receive and adopt us once for all into the church, but through the same means he preserves and protects us there."[3]

When Moses asked to see God's glory, God revealed one of his defining characteristics—He is a God who forgives (Exodus 34:6-7). We radiate His glory when we are people who forgive. A friend who is called to daily forgive the husband who abandoned her wrote:

> I become so weary of forgiving, yet my heavenly Father does not grow weary of forgiving me. Forgiving is the most godly thing any of us ever do, and if it is true forgiveness, it is an awesome work of the Holy Spirit in us. It is a work so awesome it takes my breath away. In other words, God alone forgives. When He uses my weak vessel to manifest His for-

giveness to someone in my life, His power overwhelms me. It is greater than any *experience* a believer could hope for. I find myself flying above all of life's circumstances when Christ forgives my former husband one more time through me. It is then that I am sure that with God all things are possible.

We do not deserve God's forgiveness. Forgiveness is an act of grace. Unless forgiveness flourishes in our homes, they will not be places of grace.

Forgiveness is not just an event. It is a lifestyle decision based on our view of God. When the stones were pelting Stephen's body, he did not sit down and logically determine whether or not these people deserved his forgiveness. I don't think he calculated the cost or considered the results. He had eyes only for Jesus. God's presence with him empowered him to live beyond his own ability. His knowledge of the Risen, Reigning One pushed him into grace-zone living.

Before we continue, let me give a word of clarification. Forgiveness does not necessarily mean a restoration of the relationship. Reconciliation involves repentance *and* forgiveness, and we can only be responsible for one or the other of those actions.

The need for forgiveness abounds in all of our homes, because we are sinners and we live with sinners. The grace of forgiveness that we extend to others will be in proportion to our understanding of and gratitude for the undeserved forgiveness we have received. Forgiveness flows freely in a place of grace, and the forgivers and the forgiven are richer because they live in such an environment. This kind of home is a bold witness for the Gospel. What does it look like? Two examples demonstrate the power of forgiveness.

THE INFLUENCE OF FORGIVING PARENTS

I was scheduled for the last flight out of Rochester, Minnesota. When the flight was canceled, we were given hotel vouchers. A strikingly beautiful African-American woman and I were in line together, so we shared a cab to the hotel. When I asked why she was in Rochester, she said she had made a presentation at Mayo Clinic. She asked why I was there. Her face lit up when I said I had spoken for a women's retreat in a local church. "I'm a Christian too," she said. Conversation was easy. I felt enfolded by Deforia's winsome joy and gentleness. When we arrived at the hotel, we still had much we wanted to talk about, so we had dinner together. A remarkable story unfolded.

Dr. Deforia Lane's story is told in the book *Music As Medicine*. She is resident director of music therapy at the Ireland Cancer Center and Rainbow Babies and Children's Hospital in Cleveland. She was the first music therapist given a grant to study the therapeutic effects of music on cancer patients. Her techniques have inspired hospitals across the country to begin music therapy programs.

Deforia spoke lovingly of her husband and sons and of her parents. She explained that when her parents were young adults, they had to leave their community because of racial tensions. "They saw and experienced things so horrid I would not repeat them to you," she said. "They never spoke of these experiences as I was growing up. When I was in my mid-thirties, I began to piece some things together and ask questions. It was then that I understood the radical nature of their forgiveness to those who tormented them."

Then her face brightened as she told me about being invited to sing in her parents' hometown and being presented with the key to the city. "It was shortly before my dad died. He was too sick to go with me, but I gave the key to him. He was so proud, and he hung it in their home."

I was astonished. "Do you mean he graciously accepted this gift from those who abused him?"

She smiled. "Of course—that was my daddy." She explained that there had never been any hint of bitterness. Her parents did not hold a grudge. "They did not want me to grow up in an atmosphere of hostility. I think it is because of the environment of grace that I lived in that I am free to minister to suffering people," she said.

As I looked at this radiant woman who freely embraces others in love, I saw the product of a place of grace.

THE INFLUENCE OF A FORGIVING MARRIAGE

A couple shared the following note they received from a young single woman:

> I am grateful that God brought me to your Bible study. You always receive me into your home with such warmth and love. When I look at the two of you, I see only one body fully united in Christ. To me, your marriage is the way God has commanded it to be, and you both complement each other so joyously. It has been encouraging to see such light in your marriage and to see how God is so glorified through your service and obedience. Thank you for being my teachers.

This is a powerful testimony to any Christian marriage, but it is especially so in this case. I know what the young woman does not know. Several years ago there was infidelity in this marriage. Thorough repentance and thorough forgiveness resulted in a sturdier and sweeter oneness. This young woman sees an unscorched, unscarred oneness that is an evidence of God's grace. The forgiver in this situation has shared elements of the story with me that show the multifaceted dimensions of forgiveness.

> Everything I believed was on the line. Was God big enough for this? Was His grace sufficient? Was Romans 8:28 true? Could He cause even this to work together for His glory and my good?
> I continued to follow my regular plan of Scripture reading, which included an Old Testament and a New Testament reading. A few days after the confession, I read Hebrews 12:14-15: "Make every effort to live in peace with all men and to be holy; without holiness no one will see the Lord. See to it that no one misses the grace of God and that no bitter root grows up to cause trouble and defile many." I did not want to miss the grace of God, so I begged Him not to let even a root of bitterness find a place in my heart. I

knew that I had the potential to do things far worse than my spouse had done, and that I was vulnerable to the sin of bitterness.

My Old Testament reading was Ezekiel 22:30: "I looked for a man among them who would build up the wall and stand before me in the gap on behalf of the land so I would not have to destroy it, but I found none." In my mind's eye, I could see myself standing in the gap on behalf of my own family, but also to protect the family of the person who had been involved with my spouse. I knew the Lord was calling me to pray for that family's protection even as I prayed for my own. And I knew that my response to this call would reveal my own heart. Again I begged for grace, and grace was sufficient. I stood in the gap.

Our family did not suffer the aftershocks you would expect from such an upheaval. God does give "a crown of beauty instead of ashes, the oil of gladness instead of mourning, and a garment of praise instead of a spirit of despair . . ." so that we become "oaks of righteousness, a planting of the LORD for the display of his splendor" (Isaiah 61:3).

This marriage is indeed a display of the splendor of God's grace.

Every time intact families gather and enjoy happy times at grandparents' homes, those grandparents give the gift of the fruit of forgiveness. For any marriage to survive and thrive, there will be abundant doses of repentance and forgiveness along the way. Forgiveness is costly, but not to forgive robs our children and grandchildren of an unfractured legacy.

Forgiveness will distinguish our families from all the other families on the face of the earth (Exodus 33:16). It authenticates the Gospel. I am convinced that the Christian family is one of our greatest evangelistic resources. When people see forgiving families, they know something extraordinary is going on in that home. They see something they cannot duplicate.

Forgiveness is not always as dramatic as the examples above.

What does forgiveness look like when it is tucked into everyday family life?

• It looks like the daddy who asks his children to forgive him for losing his temper.

• It looks like the little boy who can easily but sincerely say, "I'm sorry. Will you forgive me?" to his friend because he hears those words regularly from his parents.

• It looks like the wife who does not hold a grudge over forgotten birthdays because love "keeps no record of wrongs" (1 Corinthians 13:5).

• It looks like the teenage girl who is not afraid to go to her parents and say, "I am pregnant," because she lives with repentant, forgiving parents who have shown her what it means to "love each other deeply, because love covers over a multitude of sins" (1 Peter 4:8).

• It looks like the young mother who faithfully compliments her mother-in-law who rudely criticizes her. In so doing, her children absorb valuable lessons about honor and forgiveness.

• It looks like the family who prays for the neighbor child who bullies their son and for the church family that has gossiped about them (Matthew 5:44).

• It looks like the family who frequently has times of repentance when they confess their selfishness or indifference or prejudices.

True forgiveness does *not* look manipulative. I am not to forgive because I have determined that this may teach my offender a lesson. True forgiveness only has eyes for Jesus. When we see the Risen, Reigning One in His Word, we will not want anything as nonsensical as bitterness and resentment to diminish our intimacy with Him.

What does forgiveness look like? It looks like Jesus:

> *This is the covenant I will make with the house of Israel after that time, declares the Lord. I will put my laws in their minds and write them on their hearts. I will be their God, and they will be my people. No longer will a man teach his neighbor, or a man his brother, saying, "Know the Lord," because they will all know*

*me, from the least of them to the greatest. For I will forgive their
wickedness and will remember their sins no more.*

HEBREWS 8:10-12

This is a bold initiative.

Why should we live this way? Because we belong to the Risen,
Reigning One, and our overarching purpose is to glorify Him.

How can we live this way? By living in the grace zone.

What will motivate us to embrace this family value? The knowledge
that the Risen, Reigning One has forgiven us and is always with us
will develop a reverence, humility, and gratitude that will compel us
to a life of radical forgiveness.

How do we teach our children to live this way? By living this way and
by telling them over and over why we do what we do.

THE ANCIENT PATH

Here is the ancient path, the good way. Meditate on it and walk in it.

*Therefore, as God's chosen people, holy and dearly loved, clothe
yourselves with compassion, kindness, humility, gentleness and
patience. Bear with each other and forgive whatever grievances you
may have against one another. Forgive as the Lord forgave you.
And over all these virtues put on love, which binds them all
together in perfect unity. Let the peace of Christ rule in your hearts,
since as members of one body you were called to peace. And be
thankful. Let the word of Christ dwell in you richly as you teach
and admonish one another with all wisdom, and as you sing
psalms, hymns and spiritual songs with gratitude in your hearts
to God. And whatever you do, whether in word or deed, do it all
in the name of the Lord Jesus, giving thanks to God the Father
through him.*

COLOSSIANS 3:12-17

May our families embrace this mission and leave this legacy.

QUESTIONS AND ANSWERS

Q. Realistically, my wife does the majority of the parenting. I'm just not there all day as she is. What can I do to support and encourage her?

A. The dad's influence is powerful even though he's not with the kids as many hours of the day. His example can make or break everything the mother teaches all during the day. For example, she can talk about good manners, but if the dad begins eating his dessert before the person serving has been seated, the children will follow his example rather than her instruction. She can insist on good habits such as hanging the bath towel straight, putting dirty clothes in the hamper, and not leaving dishes for someone else to wash, but if Dad does these things, she is fighting a losing battle.

If children treat their mother with disrespect or indifference, Dad needs to examine his attitude and behavior toward his wife. It seems to me that children instinctively know that Dad is the head of the family, and what he *does* will reinforce or negate what Mom says.

A man who expresses appreciation to his wife for meals, does not expect her to be his maid, compliments her, and treats her with gentleness and kindness gives his wife a treasured gift and teaches his children what godly manhood looks like.

Q. A final question: When should we talk to our children about sex?

A. I encourage you to be more concerned about the context in which that conversation will take place than the actual conversation itself. The way husbands and wives treat each other, the respect they show for one another, the way they blend their gifts and graces, and the way they serve the Lord together teaches children about their own sexuality. When husbands and wives are happy and comfortable with their gender roles, they provide a healthy place to have the sex conversation. If husbands and/or wives make an issue of the physical attractiveness (or unattractiveness) of other people, they teach their children a faulty view of sex. But if they express appreciation for spiritual qualities in each other, they teach their children to value these qualities. As to the actual conversation, there is no magic time. Much will depend on the individual child and the situations and people to which the child is exposed. Ask the Lord to give you wisdom not to tell too much too soon and not to withhold information too long.

1. Read Exodus 34:6-7.
    - Meditate again on the wonder of these attributes of God.
    - Pray that you will have eyes only for Jesus and that your life will reflect the reality of the Risen, Reigning One.

2. Read 1 Corinthians 13.
    - List the characteristics of love.
    - Which of these requires a forgiving heart?

3. Read Isaiah 43:1-21 several times. List the promises that are especially meaningful to you.

4. Read Ephesians 4:29-32. Pray that you and your family will be obedient to this command.

5. Read Ephesians 5:1—6:4.

CONCLUSION

It must be evident to every person of observation that children and youth, in forming their estimate of different objects, are guided almost entirely by the opinions of those who precede them in the journey of life. A child, left to itself, would prefer the smallest coin to a bank note, and a piece of painted glass to the most valuable diamond. And how does he learn to judge more correctly? Simply by observing how objects are valued by those who are older and wiser than himself. . . . However diligently we may impart to them a knowledge of God and his works, if we do not appear to think highly of him, to love his character, to admire his works, and to prefer him to every other object, our instructions will have but very little effect. But if they hear us frequently speak of him in the glowing language of gratitude, love, and praise; if they see that we consider him as all in all; that we regard it as detestable and base to neglect him; and that the language of our conduct is, Whom have we in heaven but thee, and what is there on earth that we desire besides thee?——they will in all probability, be insensibly led to adopt, not only our opinions respecting him, but our feelings towards him. . . . To speak God's praises to the rising generation is then, if possible, even more important than to impart to them a knowledge of his works. Both, however, are necessary and should never be separated.[1]

EDWARD PAYSON

s I look back over this book, I realize that it is simply the ramblings of a grandmother. That is not an apology, for grandmothering is a good thing. Every rising generation needs to see and hear grandmothers and grandfathers lovingly engaged in commending the person and work of Jesus. Every rising generation needs to see those ahead of them applying God's truth to every part of life. This grandmother wants to give you what Elizabeth Prentiss has given me.

Elizabeth Prentiss lived from 1818 to 1878. She was the daughter of Edward Payson, whom I have quoted liberally in this book. It was said that Mrs. Prentiss grew up breathing *sanctified air.* Her father's influence is certainly evident in her writings. This daughter of a pastor also married a pastor. During adulthood she became a novelist so that she could tell "the next generation the praiseworthy deeds of the LORD, his power, and the wonders he has done" (Psalm 78:4). Her deep commitment to the family shows through every line of her splendid books. *Stepping Heavenward* is a treatise on the Christian life. *Aunt Jane's Hero* is a marriage manual of the highest order. And *The Home at Greylock* walks her readers through the parenting maze. In each of these lovely stories, there are older men and women who tenderly guide the younger generation. Listen in on a conversation from *The Home at Greylock.* Mrs. Grey's son Fred has brought his wife and first child, Kitty, for a visit. Just before they return home, he talks with his mother about Kitty.

"Well, isn't Kitty a perfect beauty?"

"She is very pretty."

"Is that all you have to say? In my eyes, she is the most beautiful child on earth. But as to her behavior, I can't say I have anything to boast of. She is a little fury when she is provoked."

"Strange, isn't it?" said Mrs. Grey.

"But, Mother, I have outgrown all that sort of thing. And it is provoking to see one's faults repeated in one's child. But you may depend upon it, we are not going to spoil Kitty. Her mother fights her out on every line of battle."

"But be cautious, Fred. This little human flower must expand elsewhere than on a battle-field. You can't begin too soon to let her see that intense, unselfish love lies at the bottom of all restraint and correction. You and Hatty are both, by nature, law-givers, and I do not doubt you will have a family of obedient children, as you ought to do. But think of the goodness as well as the severity of God when you discipline your child. Never enter upon a conflict with her without asking Him how to proceed; in this way you will avoid a thousand mistakes."

Fred colored and looked embarrassed. It had not occurred to him that a grown-up man was not quite equal to the task of training a little child; on the contrary, he had rather prided himself on his skill. . . . "Do you think there is a fair prospect of Kitty's turning out well at last?"

"Yes, my dear boy, if you will lay to heart the counsel of your mother, and part with all pride and self-reliance, and rely on Divine strength alone. Oh, that I had realized this in the early years of my married life and taken counsel of God at every step!"

"I don't see but we must go home and reconstruct our domestic life," said Fred. "We were young and strong, and of one mind; we were resolved to have an obedient child, at any cost; and of course we have prayed for her; but I am afraid not specifically enough. . . . I shall go home a wiser, but a sadder man," said Fred. "I never realized before that the work of training up a child is such an *awful* task."

"It is only awful when undertaken by a fool or a knave. You will find, as other children come to you, that rules that apply to one, fail in regard to another. What I have advised in regard to Kitzie [Kitty] may not apply in the least to your Fred, Jr., when you get that young man."

Fred Grey was worth all he had cost his mother, for his was a strong, thoughtful character. And all that she had now said to him impressed him, as it did his wife, when he repeated it to her. Poor little baby Kitty never had another battle with her resolute young parents; yet day by day she was learning obedience; day by day they were learning humility and self-control. Their love to each other and to their child grew purer and sweeter, and co-operating together in all their plans for her, her lot bid fair to be a most enviable one.²

Dear reader, I am sure you have realized that I cannot tell you how to have a home that is a place of grace. I hope you have realized that my desire is to tell you about the One who is a Haven of Grace for those who cling to Him. He is all you need. As Mrs. Prentiss said, "part with all pride and self-reliance, and rely on Divine strength alone."

I think that the Old Testament characters Hannah and David understood this. Their parental prayers are quite remarkable. They spoke so little of their offspring, but so much of their God.

A MOTHER'S PRAYER

Hannah was a woman with a broken heart because of her barrenness. The Lord opened her womb and gave her a child. When Samuel was weaned, she took him to the house of the Lord at Shiloh, presented him to Eli the priest, and said: "'I prayed for this child, and the LORD has granted me what I asked of him. So now I give him to the LORD. For his whole life he will be given over to the LORD'" (1 Samuel 1:27-28).

Then Hannah prayed and said:

> "My heart rejoices in the LORD; in the LORD my horn is lifted high. My mouth boasts over my enemies, for I delight in your deliverance. There is no one holy like the LORD; there is no one besides you; there is no Rock like our God.
>
> "Do not keep talking so proudly or let your mouth speak such arrogance, for the LORD is a God who knows, and by him deeds are weighed.
>
> "The bows of the warriors are broken, but those who stumbled are armed with strength. Those who were full hire themselves out for food, but those who were hungry hunger no more. She who was barren has borne seven children, but she who has had many sons pines away.

"The LORD brings death and makes alive; he brings down to the grave and raises up. The LORD sends poverty and wealth; he humbles and he exalts. He raises the poor from the dust and lifts the needy from the ash heap; he seats them with princes and has them inherit a throne of honor. For the foundations of the earth are the LORD's; upon them he has set the world.

"He will guard the feet of his saints, but the wicked will be silenced in darkness. It is not by strength that one prevails; those who oppose the LORD will be shattered. He will thunder against them from heaven; the LORD will judge the ends of the earth. He will give strength to his king and exalt the horn of his anointed."

1 SAMUEL 2:1-10

Scripture tells us that Hannah's son "ministered before the LORD under Eli the priest. . . . The boy Samuel grew up in the presence of the LORD" (vv. 11, 21).

A FATHER'S PRAYER

When God told King David that the task of building the temple would be given to his son, David gave this charge to Solomon: "Be strong and courageous, and do the work. Do not be afraid or discouraged, for the LORD God, my God, is with you. He will not fail you or forsake you until all the work for the service of the temple of the LORD is finished" (1 Chronicles 28:20).

Then King David spoke to the whole assembly: "My son Solomon, the one whom God has chosen, is young and inexperienced. The task is great, because this palatial structure is not for man but for the LORD God" (1 Chronicles 29:1).

David knew his son's limitations, but he knew God's limitless power.

David praised the LORD in the presence of the whole assembly, saying, "Praise be to you, O LORD, God of our father Israel, from everlasting to everlasting. Yours, O LORD, is the greatness and the power and the glory and the majesty and the splendor, for everything in heaven and earth is yours. Yours, O LORD, is the kingdom; you are exalted as head over all. Wealth and honor come from you; you are the ruler of all things. In your hands are strength and power to exalt and give strength to all. Now, our God, we give you thanks, and praise your glorious name.

"But who am I, and who are my people, that we should be able to give as generously as this? Everything comes from you, and we have given you only what comes from your hand. We are aliens and strangers in your sight, as were all our forefathers. Our days on earth are like a shadow, without hope. O LORD our God, as for all this abundance that we have provided for building you a temple for your Holy Name, it comes from your hand, and all of it belongs to you.

"I know, my God, that you test the heart and are pleased with integrity. All these things have I given willingly and with honest intent. And now I have seen with joy how willingly your people who are here have given to you. O LORD, God of our fathers Abraham, Isaac and Israel, keep this desire in the hearts of your people forever, and keep their hearts loyal to you. And give my son Solomon the wholehearted devotion to keep your commands, requirements and decrees and to do everything to build the palatial structure for which I have provided."

1 CHRONICLES 29:10-19

Scripture tells us that God appeared to Solomon and said, "Ask for whatever you want me to give you." Solomon's prayer is a fitting conclusion to this book:

"Give me wisdom and knowledge, that I may lead this people, for who is able to govern this great people of yours?"

2 CHRONICLES 1:10

We must look to God for wisdom and knowledge to lead our families, for none of us is able to govern them in our own strength. May it be said of us, as it was of the ancients:

They entered into a covenant to seek the LORD, the God of their fathers, with all their heart and soul.

2 CHRONICLES 15:12

Then our homes and our churches will be places of grace, and Christendom will be stronger and brighter as we anticipate the return of our Bridegroom to take us home.

Then I heard what sounded like a great multitude, like the roar of rushing waters and like loud peals of thunder, shouting: "Hallelujah! For our Lord God Almighty reigns. Let us rejoice and be glad and give him glory! For the wedding of the Lamb has come, and his bride has made herself ready. Fine linen, bright and clean, was given her to wear."

REVELATION 19:6-8

The Spirit and the bride say, "Come!" . . .
Come, Lord Jesus.
The grace of the Lord Jesus be with God's people.
Amen.

REVELATION 22:17, 20-21

NOTES

PART ONE

1. John Angell James, *A Help to Domestic Happiness* (London: Frederick Westley and A. H. Davis, 1833; reprinted Morgan, Penn.: Soli Deo Gloria Publications, 1995), viii.

1: THE COVENANT FAMILY

1. Abraham Kuyper, *Near Unto God* (Grand Rapids, Mich.: CRC Publications and William Eerdmans, 1997), 22.
2. Michael S. Hamilton, "The Triumph of the Praise Songs," *Christianity Today*, July 12, 1999.
3. R. C. Sproul, ed., *The New Geneva Study Bible*, note on Genesis 17:10-13 (Nashville, Tenn.: Thomas Nelson, 1995), 37.
4. Charles Hodge, *Systematic Theology*, Vol. 3 (Grand Rapids, Mich.: William Eerdmans, 1991), 555.
5. John Bunyan, *Pilgrim's Progress in Modern English* (Chicago: Moody Press, 1964), 151.
6. *Trinity Hymnal* (Atlanta, Ga.: Great Commission Publications, 1990), 4.
7. Joni Eareckson Tada, *Holiness in Hidden Places* (Nashville, Tenn.: Thomas Nelson, 1999), 38-39.

2: THREE HOMES

1. George Whitefield, ed., *The Godly Family, Essays on the Duties of Parents and Children* (Morgan, Penn.: Soli Deo Gloria Publications, 1993), 46.
2. George Grant, *Carry a Big Stick* (Elkton, Md.: Highland Books, 1996), 51.
3. John Angell James, *A Help to Domestic Happiness* (London: Frederick Westley and A. H. Davis, 1833; reprinted Morgan, Penn.: Soli Deo Gloria Publications, 1995), 11-13.
4. Ibid., vi.
5. Bryan Chapell, *Each for the Other* (Grand Rapids, Mich.: Baker Books, 1998), 13-14.
6. Eileen O'Gorman, "Life Lessons," *Leader to Leader*, ed. Benjamin K. Homan (St. Louis, Mo.: Covenant Theological Seminary, Fall 1999), 1-4.
7. Don Kistler, *A Spectacle unto God: The Life and Death of Christopher Love* (Morgan, Penn.: Soli Deo Gloria Publications, 1994), 1-3.

3: PURPOSE AND AUTHORITY

1. John Angell James, *A Help to Domestic Happiness* (London: Frederick Westley and A. H. Davis, 1833; reprinted Morgan, Penn.: Soli Deo Gloria Publications, 1995), 10.

2. The Westminster Shorter Catechism (Atlanta: Presbyterian Church in America Committee for Christian Education & Publications, 1990), Question 1.

3. Ibid., Question 2.

4. Louis Berkhof and Cornelius Van Til, *Foundations of Christian Education: Addresses to Christian Teachers*, ed. Dennis E. Johnson (Phillipsburg, N.J.: Presbyterian and Reformed Publishing Co., 1990, originally published in 1953 by William Eerdmans), 116.

5. Ibid., 3.

6. Abraham Kuyper, *Near Unto God* (Grand Rapids, Mich.: CRC Publications and William Eerdmans, 1997), 18-19.

7. *Catechism for Young Children*, Questions 1-5 (Atlanta: Presbyterian Church in America Committee for Christian Education & Publications, n.d.).

8. J. G. Vos, *The Covenant of Grace* (Pittsburgh, Penn.: Crown & Covenant Publications, reprinted by permission of Blue Banner Faith and Life, n.d.), 15.

9. Ibid., 7.

10. The Westminster Confession of Faith, VII, 1 (Atlanta: Presbyterian Church in America Committee for Christian Education & Publications, 1990), 24.

11. Berkhof and Van Til, *Foundations*, 68.

12. John H. Gerstner, *Jonathan Edwards, Evangelist* (Morgan, Penn.: Soli Deo Gloria Publications, 1995), 176, 185, 186.

13. Ibid., 173-174.

14. Don Kistler, *A Spectacle unto God: The Life and Death of Christopher Love* (Morgan, Penn.: Soli Deo Gloria Publications, 1994), 100-102.

4: MARRIAGE

1. John Angell James, *A Help to Domestic Happiness* (London: Frederick Westley and A. H. Davis, 1833; reprinted Morgan, Penn.: Soli Deo Gloria Publications, 1995), 24.

2. Edmund Clowney, "Not Many Wise," *Tabletalk*, Vol. 23, No. 7, ed. R. C. Sproul, Jr. (July 1999, Ligonier Ministries, Inc.), 57.

5: PARENTING

1. George Whitefield, ed., *The Godly Family, Essays on the Duties of Parents and Children* (Morgan, Penn.: Soli Deo Gloria Publications, 1993), 91.

2. Ibid., 77, 86-87.

3. Ibid., 87.

4. Ibid., 78-80.

5. R. Laird Harris, ed., *The Theological Wordbook of the Old Testament*, Vol. 1 (Chicago: Moody Press, 1980), 301.

6. Ibid., 282-283.

7. Louis Berkhof and Cornelius Van Til, *Foundations of Christian Education: Addresses to Christian Teachers*, ed. Dennis E. Johnson (Phillipsburg, N.J.: Presbyterian and Reformed Publishing Co., 1990, originally published in 1953 by William Eerdmans), 77.

6: RESOURCES

1. John Angell James, *A Help to Domestic Happiness* (London: Frederick Westley and A. H. Davis, 1833; reprinted Morgan, Penn.: Soli Deo Gloria Publications, 1995), 154.

2. Edward Payson, *The Complete Works of Edward Payson*, Vol. 1, comp. Asa Cummings (Hyde, Lord & Duren, 1846, reprinted Harrisonburg, Va.: Sprinkle Publications, 1987), 521.

3. The Westminster Confession of Faith, XXVI, 1 (Atlanta: Presbyterian Church in America Committee for Christian Education & Publications, 1990), 85.

4. James, *Domestic Happiness*, 128-129.

PART TWO
7: THE GLORIOUS ONE

1. Samuel Worcester, "Parental Duties Illustrated," in George Whitefield, ed., *The Godly Family: Essays on the Duties of Parents and Children* (Morgan, Penn.: Soli Deo Gloria Publications, 1993), 77.

2. R. C. Sproul, ed., "The Ascension of Jesus," in *The New Geneva Study Bible* (Nashville, Tenn.: Thomas Nelson, 1995), 1655.

3. Edward Payson, *The Complete Works of Edward Payson*, Vol. 3, comp. Asa Cummings (Hyde, Lord & Duren, 1846, reprinted Harrisonburg, Va.: Sprinkle Publications, 1987), 540-552.

8: THE JUST ONE

1. Samuel Stennett, in George Whitefield, ed., *The Godly Family: Essays on the Duties of Parents and Children* (Morgan, Penn.: Soli Deo Gloria Publications, 1993), 310.

2. John Calvin, *Institutes of the Christian Religion*, ed. John T. McNeill (Philadelphia: Westminster Press, 1960), (3.11.1) 2:37.

3. James Montgomery Boice, *Acts: An Expositional Commentary* (Grand Rapids, Mich.: Baker Books, 1997), 151.

4. The Westminster Shorter Catechism (Atlanta: Presbyterian Church in America Committee for Christian Education & Publications, 1990), Question 33.

5. Don Kistler, *A Spectacle unto God: The Life and Death of Christopher Love* (Morgan, Penn.: Soli Deo Gloria Publications, 1994), 164.

6. Edward Payson, *The Complete Works of Edward Payson*, Vol. 1, comp. Asa

Cummings (Hyde, Lord & Duren, 1846, reprinted Harrisonburg, Va.: Sprinkle Publications, 1987), 500-501.

7. Ibid., 347.

9: THE SOVEREIGN HOLY ONE

1. Edward Payson, *The Complete Works of Edward Payson*, Vol. 1, comp. Asa Cummings (Hyde, Lord & Duren, 1846, reprinted Harrisonburg, Va.: Sprinkle Publications, 1987), 530.

2. Derek Thomas, *God Delivers* (Grange Close, Faverdale North, Darlington, England: Evangelical Press, 1991), 73.

3. R. C. Sproul, ed., *The New Geneva Study Bible* (Nashville, Tenn.: Thomas Nelson, 1995), 1036.

4. Ibid., "God Delivers," 353.

5. John Frame, *Worship in Spirit and in Truth* (Phillipsburg, N.J.: Presbyterian and Reformed Publishing Co., 1996), 1-11.

6. George Grant, *The Micah Mandate: Balancing the Christian Life* (Nashville, Tenn.: Cumberland House, 1995, 1999), 10.

7. Ibid., 7-8.

10: THE RISEN, REIGNING ONE

1. John Angell James, *The Christian Father's Present to His Children* (New York: Robert Carter and Brothers, 1853; reprinted Morgan, Penn.: Soli Deo Gloria Publications, 1993), 27.

2. Sinclair Ferguson, *Daniel*, Mastering the Old Testament, Vol. 19 (Dallas: Word Publishing, 1988), 78.

3. John Calvin, *Institutes of the Christian Religion*, ed. John T. McNeill (Philadelphia: Westminster Press, 1960), (IV.1.21), 1035-1035.

CONCLUSION

1. Edward Payson, *The Complete Works of Edward Payson*, Vol. 3, comp. Asa Cummings (Hyde, Lord & Duren, 1846, reprinted Harrisonburg, Va.: Sprinkle Publications, 1987), 347-348.

2. Elizabeth Prentiss, *The Home at Greylock* (New York: Anson D. F. Randolph & Co., 1876), 89-93.

The Lord God said, "It is not good for the man to be alone.
I will make a helper suitable for him."
GENESIS 2:18

God had a distinctive plan and purpose when He created men
and women different. *By Design* is a joyous celebration of that
profound fact. But it is more. This uplifting and practical intro-
duction to God's wonderful design for the woman as a "helper"
will challenge you to explore the significance of your distinctives
and biblical calling. And it is a rallying cry to the church to equip
and mobilize one of its greatest resources—you.

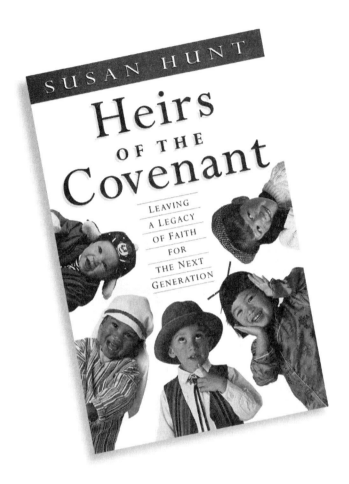

Today's fragmented culture is grasping for direction and meaningful values; the church must offer more than secular educational
methods sprinkled with Bible stories. True Christian education
can draw families together in committed, caring relationships that
extend beyond age groups and into community life. Susan Hunt
explores what happens when, day by day, week by week, generation by generation, the church leads its people into the privileges
and responsibilities of covenant living. This practical plan will
encourage you to fulfill your calling to leave a legacy of faith for
the next generation—and to live for Christ today.

The Titus 2 Model
For Women Mentoring Women

SPIRITUAL
MOTHERING

SUSAN HUNT

In the second chapter of Titus, Paul teaches that older women are to be godly examples so that they can train the younger women. *Spiritual Mothering* will encourage you to put Paul's instructions into action. Throughout its pages the vision of women mentoring women is shared clearly. Using both biblical and modern-day examples, the studies and stories here illustrate the principle of Titus 2. Each chapter of this helpful and dynamic resource concludes with a practical application so that women may begin nurturing these important relationships.

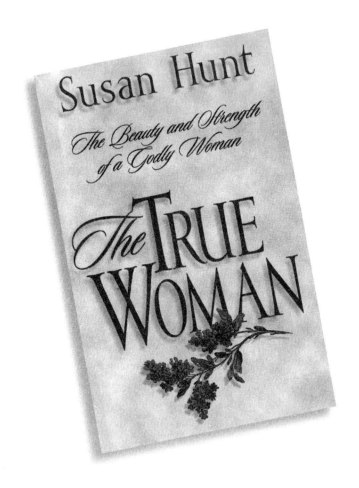

Society says, "Be a new woman. Do things your way. Take control of your life." But God calls you to be a *true* woman—a woman who reflects Christ in all of life regardless of the circumstances, who makes an impact in her home and community by her virtue, wisdom, dignity, and faith. Discover how to develop a biblically shaped and Spirit-driven character through this encouraging book. It will set your heart on fire and excite you about the unique opportunity you have as a godly woman to make a difference for eternity.

Every time a child delights in a Bible story or memorizes a verse or learns something new about who God is, that little one has taken another step toward coming to know God and wanting to live for Him. These entertaining and insightful books use stories of everyday situations that kids face to illustrate and apply scriptural principles and passages. They are a fun way for adults to systematically teach children the truths of the faith—and help them integrate those truths in a way that finds expression at home, at school, and with friends. For kids ages 3 to 8.

My ABC Bible Verses
Big Truths for Little Kids